Praise for Twins in Session

"Dr. Joan Friedman draws on her experiences as a twins' therapist to animate *Twins in Session* with her lively prose, interesting case studies, and clear and concise explanations of psychoanalytic therapies. This is an important book for any clinical mental health professional who treats twins."
—*Ann E. Cudd, Dean, College of Arts & Sciences, Boston University*

"*Twins in Session* is an essential buy for twins and their families. It shines a light on the different relationship dynamics between twins, their friends, their partners, and their family. This book will help thousands to better understand their bonds and relationships and move forward in a healthier and even more rewarding way."
—*Keith Reed, CEO, Twins and Multiple Births Association (TAMBA), Southampton, United Kingdom*

"Dr. Friedman aims to educate and enlighten other health professions who, through lack of experience with twins, do not appreciate the intricacies of twin relationships. *Twins in Session* also provides fascinating insights that go beyond the common misconception that all twin pairs are alike and get along fine. Overall, a fascinating and easy-to-read book."
—*Dr. Jeffrey Craig, medical researcher and Associate Professor, Deakin University, Geelong, Australia*

"*Twins in Session* offers a rare glimpse into the extraordinary challenges that twins encounter. An enlightening read for twins, families with twins, and professionals working with twins."
—*Nancy L. Segal, PhD, Professor of Psychology, California State University, Fullerton, and author of* Born Together—Reared Apart *and* Accidental Brothers

"*Twins in Session* was so absorbing that I couldn't put it down! Those who work with twins should have this book as an essential reference. Reading this book was like having a master class with an expert in my field. I cannot praise this book more highly."

—*Audrey Sandbank, family psychotherapist and twin specialist, Surrey, United Kingdom, and editor of* Twin and Triplet Psychology

"*Twins in Session* is a must-read for all mental health practitioners who work with twins. Dr. Friedman brings the fascinating internal worlds of twins to life in a down-to-earth style that doesn't compromise on complexity."

—*Ruth Simon, PhD, psychoanalytic psychotherapist and twin parenting consultant*

"*Twins in Session* reveals professional and personal insights only Joan Friedman could deliver. This book should be referenced by every therapist and required reading for all students of human behavior."

—*Eve-Marie Arce, EdD, author of* Twins and Supertwins

"*Twins in Session* will answer many questions that adult twins ask today. Dr. Friedman reveals how multilayered twinship is for both twins and nontwins and confronts some of the preconceived ideas held by a nontwin world."

—*Sirpa Rosendahl, PhD, Senior Lecturer, Mälardalen University, Västerås, Sweden*

"*Twins in Session* is a thoughtful, insightful, and informative analysis of twins' experiences, inner feelings, and insights uncovered through therapy. I highly recommend this book to adult twins, therapists, and all others interested in multiple births."

—*Eileen M. Pearlman, PhD, psychotherapist; Director, TwInsight; and coauthor of* Raising Twins

"Dr. Friedman masterfully enriches our journey toward a more profound understanding of twin relationships. *Twins in Session* is a joy, inspiring both reflection and confidence in working with twins. I recommend this jewel."

—*María del Pilar Grazioso, PhD, Director, Doctoral Program in Applied Psychology, Universidad del Valle de Guatemala, and Cocoordinator, Proyecto Aiglé Guatemala, Guatemala City*

"*Twins in Session* beautifully and thoughtfully captures the inner lives of twins. Dr. Friedman masterfully highlights the importance of clinical sensitivity to key developmental, relational, and identity issues facing twins, which makes this book essential reading for clinicians who treat twins."

—*Michael Rothman, PhD, psychologist specializing in twins and Assistant Clinical Professor, Icahn School of Medicine at Mount Sinai*

"Dr. Joan A. Friedman has developed innovative treatment approaches to help readers understand twinship and help twins gain a sense of being separate from each other rather than suffer from severe self-deficits and incompleteness."

—*Salomon Grimberg, MD, child psychiatrist*

"This is the book we have been waiting for! *Twins in Session* will be invaluable to therapists working with adult twins. I loved reading every page."

—*Coks Feenstra, child psychologist specializing in twins, Valencia, Spain, and author of* El Gran Libro de los Gemelos

"A highly insightful and thought-provoking book and a must-read for any psychotherapist working with twins. Joan Friedman highlights twins' unique developmental challenges with compassion and deeply felt understanding."

—*Judith Muschel, LMFT, psychotherapist and identical twin*

"*Twins in Session* is profound and gives deep insights into the inner landscape of twins. Very useful for psychotherapists, twins, and others who want to understand twins."

—*Dr. Regina van Gelderan, psychoanalyst, Amsterdam, Netherlands*

"*Twins in Session* provides a deep and sophisticated understanding of twinship dynamics and debunks common misunderstandings about how twins experience themselves, their relationships, and their world. A must-read for every therapist!"

—*Sophie Wasson, PsyD, psychologist, Harvard-Westlake School*

"Dr. Friedman provides an invaluable resource for seasoned and aspiring clinicians alike. Rich in both theory and case studies, *Twins in Session* provides insight into the unique psychosocial experience of twins and how clinicians can best address their emotional and relational needs in therapy."

—*Catherine Goldhouse, LCSW, clinical social worker, McLean Hospital, and spouse of a twin*

Twins in Session

Other Books by Joan A. Friedman, PhD

Emotionally Healthy Twins:
A New Philosophy for Parenting Two Unique Children

The Same but Different:
How Twins Can Live, Love, and Learn to Be Individuals

Twins in Session
Case Histories in Treating Twinship Issues

Joan A. Friedman, PhD

ROCKY PINES PRESS

Los Angeles, California

Copyright © 2018 by Joan A. Friedman

All rights reserved. No part of this publication may be reproduced, distributed, or transmitted in any form or by any means, including photocopying, recording, or other electronic or mechanical methods, without the prior written permission of the publisher, except in the case of brief quotations embodied in critical reviews and certain other noncommercial uses permitted by copyright law. For permission requests, write to the publisher, addressed "Attention: Permissions Coordinator," at the address below.

Rocky Pines Press
11870 Santa Monica Blvd., #106-666
Los Angeles, CA 90025
www.rockypinespress.com

Ordering Information
Quantity sales. Special discounts are available on quantity purchases by corporations, associations, and others. For details, contact the "Special Sales Department" at the address above.

Orders by US trade bookstores and wholesalers. Please contact BCH: (800) 431-1579 or visit www.bookch.com for details.

Printed in the United States of America

Cataloging-in-Publication Data
Names: Friedman, Joan A., author.
Title: Twins in session : case histories in treating twinship issues / Joan A. Friedman, PhD.
Description: Includes index and bibliographical references. | Los Angeles, CA: Rocky Pines Press, 2018.
Identifiers: ISBN 978-0-9893464-5-0 | LCCN
Subjects: LCSH Twins—Psychology—Case Studies. | Sibling attachment. | Therapist and patient. | BISAC PSYCHOLOGY / Psychotherapy / Couples & Family | PSYCHOLOGY / Psychotherapy / Counseling | FAMILY & RELATIONSHIPS / Siblings
Classification: LCC BF723.T9 F75 2018 | DDC 155.44/4—dc23

First Edition

22 21 20 19 18   10 9 8 7 6 5 4 3 2 1

Cover photo by Amalia Ulman, Excellences & Perfections 3/3/2016,(# itsjustdifferent)(2015). Image Courtesy of the Artist and Arcadia Missa.

Disclaimer: This publication contains the opinions and ideas of its author. It is intended to provide helpful and informative material on the subject matter covered. It is sold with the understanding that the author and publisher are not engaged in rendering professional services in the book. If the reader requires expert assistance or counseling is needed, the services of a professional should be sought. Every attempt has been made to present accurate and timely information. Nothing contained herein should constitute an absolute with regard to this subject matter or be considered a substitute for legal, medical, or psychological advice. The author and publisher assume neither liability nor responsibility to any person or entity with respect to any direct or indirect loss or damaged caused, or alleged to be caused by the information contained herein, or for errors, omissions, inaccuracies, or any other inconsistency within these pages, or for unintentional slights against people or organizations.

The names and any identifying details of people associated with events described in this book have been changed. Any similarity to actual persons is coincidental.

To Robert

Contents

	Preface ix
Chapter 1	Twin Attachment 1
Chapter 2	Excessive Interdependence 25
Chapter 3	Good Twin/Bad Twin 47
Chapter 4	Caretaker/Cared-for 67
Chapter 5	Crisis of Identity 87
Chapter 6	Replacement Twins 109
Chapter 7	Significant Other versus Twin. 127
Chapter 8	Being a Twin's Therapist 149
	Notes 167
	Index 171
	About the Author 177

Preface

When I began my research on the psychology of twinship over thirty years ago, most of the literature was written in a language inaccessible to the nonacademic reader, and many psychoanalysts writing about twins in treatment focused on examining extreme abnormalities. Understanding the role that twinship can play in causing serious emotional dysfunction is certainly important; however, the extreme case studies I came across in my research did not mirror the issues that I struggled with in my own twinship and that I knew other twins grappled with as well.

The relative lack of published analysis and case histories reflective of more common twinship issues motivated me to write *The Same but Different*, a book for adult twins. My objective was to offer adult twins the opportunity to learn about the expectable—rather than the extreme—developmental issues that often arise as a consequence of being a twin, as well as the positive and negative impact that a twinship can have on one's emotional health, relationships, and sense of self.

As my therapy practice grew and increasing numbers of twins began contacting me to provide help with their twinship-related problems, I realized that many of my clients had experienced difficulties with previous therapists who were unfamiliar with twin psychology. In fact, a number of clients relayed how a therapist had misinterpreted or misunderstood what was going on in their lives and had inaccurately characterized what it meant to be a twin.

My clients' relief at finding a therapist who understands their issues inspired me to write this book—*Twins in Session*—for mental health professionals who may be treating a twin or may be called upon to do so in the future. As a result of the increase in assisted reproductive technology over the last thirty to forty years, the birth rate of twins has essentially doubled, increasing the need for therapists to become educated in the psychological issues that concern this subgroup of the population.

This book also debunks the ongoing myths about twins. With the advent of social media, people have expanded access to stories that either idealize twins or promulgate bizarre notions about twins. Although such superficial and erroneous twin-related narratives have long been present in novels, on television, and in movies, with the internet there is now an even greater need to demystify the twinship experience and elucidate the very real issues common to twins.

Therapists need to understand the core challenges that twins face growing up as a pair and how their unique experience of having a same-age sibling influences who they become as adults and how they manage their lives and relationships. With adult twins, as with all individuals, therapists need to examine their development retrospectively. That is, we need to understand how twins' early experiences, including those related to their twinship, have impacted their adult lives.

The case histories in this book highlight particular twinship issues that arise in therapy, how they are understood by both the therapist and the client, and how such issues can be addressed by them as a team. It is my hope that *Twins in Session* provides mental health professionals the opportunity to see their twin client not as a singleton but through the illuminating and fascinating lens of twinship.

Acknowledgments

Dr. Estelle Shane has been my psychological anchor for more than two decades. She is a colleague, a mentor, a teacher, and a friend. I am indebted to her for helping me cultivate and celebrate my ambitions and goals.

CHAPTER 1

Twin Attachment

A concerned mother called me in a panic. Her eighteen-year-old son Nick, who graduated at the top of his high school class and had recently entered college, was in crisis. Just a few weeks earlier he told her he was doing well in his classes, loved the campus, and had already made a few friends. But in a recent email he revealed that he had brain fog, couldn't concentrate, and couldn't do his work. Nothing like this had ever happened to him, and he didn't understand what was going on. His visit to a college counselor provided little insight or benefit. The counselor listened while Nick recited his symptoms—intense anxiety, inability to focus, sleeplessness—and assured him that these were very common among entering freshmen. Living apart from their parents for the first time, she told him, many first-year students initially have trouble managing on their own. She offered some advice that might help him relax and fall asleep more easily.

Nick's sense that he was falling apart did not subside. Understandably, his difficulties were the reason for his mother's concern. Aware of my psychotherapeutic specialty, she contacted me. I specialize in twin issues. Her son is a twin.

Nick's distress was distinct from that of a nontwin (or singleton) adjusting to being on one's own for the first time. Certainly many young people entering college away from home go through a period of adjustment; however, Nick was confronting something far more jarring than an adjustment to college. He was undergoing a genuine crisis of identity. For the first time in his life, he was living apart from his twin, and he didn't simply miss his brother as a nontwin might. Without his brother, Nick really did not know who he was. Although he couldn't articulate it to the college counselor, he felt as if he was lacking a part of himself and he didn't know how to function without that missing piece. Off balance, scared, and unable to engage with his studies as he had previously, he was not the person he knew himself to be. He didn't recognize these new, uncomfortable feelings and was thrown into panic mode.

Since Nick had no experience being in the world as an autonomous self and he had been related to as part of a couple throughout his childhood, his perspective on his role and function in the dyad had informed his identity. His experience exemplifies why separation for twins can be a crisis. A therapist who is unfamiliar with twin issues may not fully comprehend the complexity and intensity of that crisis.

Not every twin experiences such severe anxiety when separating from his or her same-age sibling. Many of those who do have grown up with inadequate opportunities to form a secure attachment with their primary caregiver; instead, they have developed a uniquely dependent attachment to the most available person in their familial environment: their twin. In fact, the core issue underlying the various psychological problems that twins typically bring to therapy is an unhealthy, yet culturally sanctioned, twin attachment.

Attachment Theory and Beyond

Psychoanalyst John Bowlby, founder of attachment theory, theorized that an infant's need for physical and emotional security engenders compelling behaviors that prompt the primary caregiver to respond. A baby's cry, smile, or clinginess signals to the parent a particular need, which then provokes a nurturing response. In her article "Can Attachment Theory Explain All Our Relationships?" Bethany Saltman concisely summarized Bowlby's theory: "At the heart of the attachment system is a primitive kind of call and response that keeps the species alive."[1]

Donald Winnicott's model of mother-child attachment involves two important concepts: *primary maternal preoccupation* and *going on being*. Winnicott maintained that a baby comes into the world as an omnipotent being and whenever he needs something, he is attended to by his mother, who is attuned to his needs and committed to fulfilling them. Having just experienced pregnancy and childbirth, the mother is in a state of maternal preoccupation and makes herself fully available to her child. The baby thus realizes that there is an "other" who is consistently available to him to meet all his needs. As the baby repeatedly experiences his needs being met, and as the "good enough mother" begins to reconnect to parts of her own life apart from the baby, he develops the ability to be alone, without his mother, for short periods and to exist in a state of going on being.[2]

Winnicott asserted that this capacity to be alone means that the baby understands that somewhere outside himself is one reliable someone who is intimately connected to him, who responds to his cues, and who knows what he needs. During this developmental process, the baby progresses from a state of omnipotence and being essentially merged with his mother to a state in which he has the capacity to temporarily *go on being* without her.

For the baby to reach the going on being state, a healthy attachment must occur, meaning that the parent is attuned to what the infant needs; recognizes the signals of hunger, discomfort, anxiety, and so on; and attends to those physical and emotional needs.

Saltman succinctly characterizes the mother-child attachment as "Separate, connect. Separate, connect" and points out that current research underscores its impact on adult problems:

Separate, connect. Separate, connect. It's the primal dance of finding ourselves in another, and another in ourselves. Researchers believe this pattern of attachment, assessed as early as one year, is more important than temperament, IQ, social class, and parenting style to a person's development. A boom in attachment research now links adult attachment insecurity with a host of problems, from sleep disturbances, depression, and anxiety to a decreased concern with moral injustice and less likelihood of being seen as a "natural leader."[3]

Dr. Karlen Lyons-Ruth, professor of psychology at Harvard Medical School, suggested reframing the first two years of life as an *attachment-individuation* process rather than an attachment-separation process. Beatrice Beebe and Frank M. Lachmann summarize Lyons-Ruth's concept in their book *Infant Research and Adult Treatment*:

> The toddler's optimal development includes affection, using the parent as a resource for help, vigorous pursuit of contact-comfort with a parent when under stress, and the assertion of initiative and opposition without the fear of rejection. Thus the child's developmental process should be assessed by the degree to which patterns of affect regulation remain warm and mutual. At the same time, they should facilitate the child's pursuit of goals and initiative. This model of development emphasizes assertive relatedness rather than separation to achieve autonomy.[4]

In their book, based on their infant-mother observational research, Beebe and Lachmann refer to the importance of mother and baby "co-constructing" their intimate connection by way of their facial and vocal interactions. They emphasize that this is an implicit, nonverbal interactive process—a mutual influence system contextualized by each partner.

Asserting that they view autonomy and relatedness as simultaneously co-constructed, they offer this explanation:

> We reconceptualize autonomy as emerging from "good-enough" interactive regulation. Likewise, we see interactive regulation in the

optimal range as emerging from "good-enough" self-regulation of both partners. Rather than seeing autonomy and relatedness as two separate poles, we see both as simultaneously co-constructed.[5]

In a normal mother-infant interaction, the mother has the time, space, and capacity to engage in such mutual influencing and to be fully attentive to her child's emotional needs. A mother who is dependably engaged in meeting the needs of her baby generally feels satisfaction and gratification about her maternal role and responsibilities. She feels that she's doing a good job, being a good enough mother. But how is the mother-baby dynamic altered when there are two babies?

Mother and Babies, Interrupted

With two babies, a mother may feel that she is never a good enough parent because her experience is that she is constantly falling short, never able to meet the demands of two babies at once. How does an overwhelmed mother manage to have primary maternal preoccupation with two babies? And how do two same-age siblings accomplish the developmental task of learning to go on being when they are aware that they are not the lone baby and when they are rarely, if ever, given the opportunity to be alone?

In her article "There Is No Such Thing as a Baby: Early Psychic Development in Twins," Ruth Simon explains why mothers and twins don't fit into Winnicott's model of mother-child attachment.

> The psychological experience of being a twin is organized by being part of a group from the moment of birth . . . and even before. The other twin creates a threesome that interrupts the experience of unity with the mother well before there are three separate people involved. For this reason, the infant twin psychically experiences a mother who is never his or hers alone and the twin doesn't come into one's own sense of self and subjectivity through differentiation from just the mother in the same way that single babies do. Instead, the twin comes into being in a social group that includes the mother,

the burgeoning self, and another burgeoning self that is "not me" but is "like me." This has a profound impact on the internal world of the twin, which will always include a sense of a social context in addition to coming to include a sense of self.[6]

While Winnicott emphasizes the importance of learning to go on being, a twin generally goes on being with his or her twin. A twin baby experiences always or nearly always being with another baby and thus does not have the opportunity to go on being alone. Although an essential developmental task is to learn to tolerate separation from the primary person to whom the child is attached, the task cannot be wholly accomplished when a "not me" is in a position of primary importance and is always close by—namely, the child's twin.

In addition to the lack of experience of going on being alone, a twin also faces the unique circumstance of being impinged upon or interrupted by the other twin. He witnesses the other baby getting his needs attended to while the first twin's are not. So the second twin is perceived as distracting the mother from her engagement with the first twin, impinging on his time with her, and interrupting his own mother-baby attachment. And when the mother turns to focus on the first twin, he then experiences the reverse: he is impinging upon his twin. So he internalizes being both the interrupted and the interrupter. Ruth Simon explains:

> Each twin's need to have the mother available to help her or him progress through their developmental stages is in direct conflict with—and therefore an interruption of—the other twin's needs to do the same. As such, the other twin is experienced as an interruption to these important tasks, and, more important, the twins each experience him- or herself as an impingement. It is a wholly unique experience in the lives of twins to experience the self as an impingement in another's development.[7]

Since twins are always attached to either their twin or their mother, they experience themselves in a social context—connected to each other, connected to each other and to the mother, or vying with the other baby for the crucial connection to the mother.

The mother's experience of attaching to her babies is also interrupted by one or the other twin. She is constantly trying to balance attuning to one with attending to the other. Her attempt to psychologically internalize two babies is a challenge at best, as her process of attaching to one baby is continually interrupted by the need to focus on the other. So interruption occurs on all sides of the mother-babies triadic attachment.

In addition, the internal development of a twin identity is based on how each baby experiences attachment to the mother and to the other baby. As Simon points out, a crucial piece of the babies-and-mother attachment process is how the mother internalizes her two infants. Although she may believe that she is encountering each as an individual child, she also likely internalizes them together, as a set of twins. This resonates within both babies, leading to their experiencing themselves as a "we" in the mother's eyes and in their own:

> The mother's preoccupation with two rather than one baby is an internal psychic phenomenon that changes how she holds (concretely and metaphorically) each of the babies. They are not just individuals yet in her mind and so they experience themselves through her experience of them as a dyad. Infants' sense of feeling real develops, in part, through the experience of the mother's gaze. The dyadic mental hold of the mother changes how twin babies come to experience themselves. Whereas an individual baby constitutes the mother's entire psychic universe, the individual twin is never the mother's whole universe. They are each "baby and mother," "babies and mother," and "baby and baby." Because the mother's internal experience includes the fact that the twins are a twosome, it is also the experience of "twosomeness" that is available for internalization. For twins, this translates to a deep psychic experience of "we-ness" that is fundamentally different from that of single babies.[8]

So the process of attachment between a mother and two same-age babies is multilayered. It often starts with the mother meaning to attach to each baby as an individual child but is impacted by the impracticality of attending to two same-age infants, as well as the mother's internalization of her two babies as "the twins." At the same time, not only is each baby's attachment to the mother impinged upon and interrupted by the other twin, but the two babies develop a unique attachment to each other, which can make the mother feel excluded or superfluous.

Twin-to-Twin Attachment

Justifiably, mothers of twins are emotionally and physically overwhelmed. Unless the babies are coparented and nurtured by a partner or full-time caregiver, the mother needs periodic relief from her daunting responsibility to care for and attach to two babies at once. What often happens is that, cognizant of how pleasantly the twins are relating to each another, the mother may retreat from attaching to one or both children in the belief that they are attuned to each other and able to soothe and please each another. She may even believe that since the twin babies seem to make each other happy, their bonding to each another is more important than connecting with the parent. Watching their babies coo and smile at each other and happily amuse each other, parents are often lulled into believing that twin bonding is the very experience twin children need most.

Parents are generally unaware that their twins' sibling-to-sibling attachment, which may be prompted by a conscious or unconscious withdrawal by the parent, is also enhanced by a cultural belief that I refer to as the *twin mystique*. Our culture's idealization of the twin relationship is so entrenched that it is rarely questioned or examined. People assume that twins are soul mates for life who feel closer to each other than to anyone else; that in utero and during childhood they share a mystical union that far surpasses their relationships with parents, friends, and other siblings; and that as adults, their twin bond is more indestructible than their relationship with a mate. Not only is this twin connection assumed to be unbreakable, but it is revered and appreciated by the culture and by the parents of twins. Twins are said to be fortunate to have a lifetime partner who innately understands and unequivocally supports them.

As sociologist Elizabeth Stewart affirms, such cultural mythologizing leads to an insoluble dilemma for twins: they are expected to be individuals while society glamorizes and perpetuates their twinness. In her book, *Twins in Society*, author Kate Bacon references Stewart's assumption regarding a twinship paradox—namely, that twins are confronted with and required to fulfill contradictory cultural expectations:

> Twins, epitomized through the stereotype of identical twins, are constructed as interdependent "soul mates" who are "carbon copies" of each other and do "everything together." . . . Twins therefore face a series of intensified contradictions: whilst they are expected to be the same, they are expected to become different; whilst they are expected to be together and close, they are expected to become independent.[9]

The twin mystique endures because the notion that two individuals are so effortlessly and intimately linked represents a human longing for such a partnership, and buying into the myth represents a universal desire to never be abandoned or alone. Although twins do have an innate emotional closeness, a sense of inseparability is also externally imposed on them by their culture and family.

Parents may feel that they are doing nothing wrong in abdicating their parental role by allowing their twin children to, in effect, nurture themselves. In fact, they often feel gratified and proud that their twins are getting along so well and enjoying each other's company. This idea—that twins will always have each other, that they effortlessly communicate both verbally and nonverbally, that they want to spend all their time together, and that they intuitively know how to nurture each other—leads to the notion that twins are the most important people in each other's lives and that they are attached to each other in a way that is even more significant than the parent-child attachment. Acceding to this belief may lead parents to leave twins to themselves to connect with each other, which can result in the parents feeling physically relieved but emotionally excluded.

A parent of singletons doesn't have to deal with the parental exclusion factor. A parent of twins, however, needs not only to understand the dynamic of twin bonding but also to avoid feeling excluded by making sure that she attaches to each baby as an individual. Otherwise, she may feel so abandoned and helpless that she decides to give up on forging a primary attachment with either or both babies.

When twins are more attached to their same-age sibling than to their parent, they miss out on fulfilling a crucial need: to be fully attached to an adult who is attuned to them and knows how to be empathic, caring, comforting, and loving. They are missing the consistent presence of someone older and wiser whom they can respect and trust to attend to their needs and whom they will want to please. When a parent consciously or unconsciously abdicates that role and twins turn to each other instead, the children will want to please each other, but they obviously lack the emotional skills or maturity to attune to or fulfill the needs of their same-age sibling. As psychotherapist Vivienne Lewin writes, "The twinning, while comforting, is not a developmental bond."[10]

Twins whose primary attachment is to each other do not have the benefit of an attachment with a primary caregiver who can help them identify, articulate, and fulfill their needs. As these twins grow up, they may deny or be unaware of their own needs because they have been so focused on the needs of their twin. Their early childhood experience is characterized by trying to soothe, take care of, and please their twin. They are attached to that sibling, but the attachment is a disordered one, a poor substitute for a healthy attachment to a parent.

Audrey Sandbank stresses why twins' attachment to each another is not only insufficient for their psychological development but deleterious to their emotional growth:

> The projection, introjection and identification with the mother by the twin may be blurred in the absence of a consistent "mirror" and instead the twin may become an additional mirror, though one that is unable to contain and reframe the child's emotions. . . . [The] desire for emotional sustenance from the co-twin can become a lifelong dependency.[11]

Many parents of twins believe that a strong bond between their two same-age children is developmentally and psychologically healthy, a phenomenon to be heralded as a positive sign. But while friendship between siblings is always a benefit, when that connection is each twin's primary attachment, it is not a healthy sign. It may signal that one or both twins' emotional connection to their parent is weak and that they are therefore deficient in the focused, loving attention and guidance that they require from a primary caregiver.

A mother of two-year-old twins in one of my parenting groups commented: "I love seeing my little boys playing together so nicely. It makes me feel like they're really connected and that they'll grow up to be best friends." This mom and many like her feel pride and gratification, which is almost like a badge of honor, when they witness their twins "in their own world," loving each other so intensely. It means that they have done an amazing job as parents. The concern is that such sibling closeness may supersede a parent-child attachment.

Parents need to know that twin-to-twin attachment should never be a substitute for a parent-child attachment. Although parenting twins is indeed a unique and challenging situation, parents must work really hard to develop an individual attachment to each of their same-age children. When this bond exists, children reap the benefits of feeling securely connected to the loving adult who is their primary caregiver.

Attached to One More Than the Other

A mother of twins may bond with one baby more than the other, or to the exclusion of the other, and this may occur for a number of reasons. The mother may be drawn to the baby who seems to need her more or who responds more effusively when picked up, held, or cooed to. Being needed by her baby may play into the mother's need to be needed. Conversely, she may prefer the baby who seems more self-sufficient, doesn't require as much attention, or doesn't cry very often. Perhaps the mother is needy herself and admires the calmer baby's seeming self-reliance. Or maybe she shares the baby's more relaxed temperament and feels more comfortable with this twin than with the twin who seems to demand more.

A mother's inclination toward one child or the other is related to her own character, personality, and personal history. If the mother is an extrovert and she has an introverted twin, she may prefer the extrovert. Or she may find the introvert more interesting or challenging and try to draw out that child. The challenge becomes how to attune to each child separately, fulfilling the needs of each without becoming prejudiced, guilty, or conflicted about having different feelings for the children.

When a parent is unable to attach to one twin for whatever reason, that child may respond by turning away from the parent and seeking emotional sustenance elsewhere. For example, one mom told me she looked forward to taking her four-year-old daughters out separately to have one-on-one time with them, which is always a good idea. However, one little girl always wants to go on the outings and the other one doesn't. The mother told me, "I'm just going to go with the one who wants to go with me and let the other one stay with the nanny." I asked her, "Why are you giving up?"

It turns out that she actually likes the fact that her other four-year-old prefers to stay with the nanny because she is insufficiently attached to this twin and prefers the company of the twin who enjoys their time together. I explained to this mom that her reticent little girl probably does not want to go out with her one-on-one because she is angry that the mother is overly attached to the other twin, the one who *wants* to be with her. The mother acknowledged that she had not fully understood the disparity between her attachment to the preferred twin and the lack of attachment to the other. The other piece to this particular attachment scenario is that the mom confided that she feels rejected by the daughter who is more attached to the nanny. Because she didn't want to deal with those feelings of rejection, she was ready to give in and abdicate her responsibility toward her angry little girl.

When parents of twins are unaware that they are more closely attached to one twin or are unable to acknowledge that disparity, it can place an undue burden on one or both siblings. For example, a client reported that one of her thirteen-year-old twins, the more dominant and social of the two, did not want to go to the same high school as her sister. Rather than listening to the reasons why this daughter felt that she needed to separate from her sister at this point in her school career, the mom begged the girl to be okay with the same-school arrangement. Because of her closer attachment to this daughter than to the less social one, the mom spoke to her as a girlfriend rather than as a mom, pressuring the preferred daughter to collude with her instead of taking both girls' needs into consideration.

Of course, when parents of singletons are more attached to one of their children than to the others, it can lead to consequences as well. But with twins (and other multiples), the inequality of parental attachment can result in unique psychological implications, especially with regard to competition and comparison between twins and excessive interdependence. Therapists must be aware of how this scenario may have played out in the early life of twin clients.

Twin Attachment to Fathers or Second Parents

When twins become part of the family, the father or a second parent (a male or female friend, relative, or same-sex partner) generally takes on a more active role than with a singleton. The reasons for this are obvious: two babies require a second adult caregiver, not only to provide another pair of hands but to focus individual love and attention on one baby at a time. Simon refers to this significant role:

> [The father or second parent] . . . provides the baby with some psychic experience of being the only baby held in mind by another who is not preoccupied with another baby. This experience is of utmost importance in the child's ability to sort out the complicated world of me/not me relations.[12]

One twin may want to be with only one parent, the other with the other. When this is the case, parents have asked me, "Why is this happening?" This situation probably occurs because the babies have "chosen sides" to feel that there is one person to whom they can be securely attached. The babies are aware that they are in competition for their parents' attention, and they want something that they don't have to share with the other.

Some coparents agree that one parent will take primary responsibility for baby X and the other for baby Y as a way for them to cope with a challenge that is extremely difficult to handle on one's own. While such divided parenting is understandable, each parent needs to make time for each baby, as daunting as that may be. Not only is giving children the power to choose sides psychologically unhealthy, but developing an attachment between each parent and each twin is crucially important. Although parents are justifiably overwhelmed, and while choosing to attach to only one child each may make life easier for both parents, problems arise when they do so.

When a twin is attached to only one parent, that child might routinely demand, "I only want to go to the park with Dad (or Mom)." While it's perfectly fine if twins have a fluid attachment to each of their parents, preferring one on a particular day and the other during a certain outing, when attachments and preferences become concretized, fighting between siblings ensues and parents have a tendency to give in. So what began as a one-parent-only attachment becomes an ongoing power struggle.

Although parents of twins may intend to forge close attachments to both children, their need to provide equal experiences for both children can undermine their best intentions. I recently spoke at a parents-of-twins conference about the importance of alone time. A woman raised her hand to voice her concern about the unevenness of the alone time experiences that she and her husband were providing for their twin daughters: "My husband and I both have time alone with each twin, but the quality of our time together with the kids is vastly different. When one of our daughters is with me, we go to the children's museum or the park or the zoo, but my husband's time with one of them amounts to ice cream and TV. We're not giving our girls equal experiences. They have a much more worthwhile experience with me. When they're with him, they're not getting anything out of it."

This feeling by parents that twins must always be treated equally, rather than allowing them to have different experiences, is common. But parents need to acknowledge and accept that parent-child experiences are not necessarily going to be the same for each twin. I try to emphasize that simply spending alone time with a parent, even if it's in front of the TV with a bowl of ice cream, has value. What is especially important for twins is facilitating the attachment with each parent. It's not about making the alone times equal; it's about making them happen.

Again, as Ruth Simon points out, twins provide the father or second parent a much more important role than they might have with a singleton. Although sharing the parenting role is a wonderful opportunity for dads or second parents of twins, many mothers don't take advantage of it because they feel that the other parent isn't doing a good enough job. But setting standards for how a parent should engage with his or her child is not the point; what's crucial is the one-on-one connection.

A Twin's Unique Attachment History

A therapist treating a twin must discover the twin's attachment history by ascertaining the nature of the twin's attachment to the parents and to his or her twin and how those relationships played out in his or her early life. The fundamental reality in a twin's family history is that, unlike singletons, twins grow up in a social grouping from day one. Rather than a dyadic relationship with the mother, a twin's earliest experiences, as Simon points out, consist of *baby and mother, babies and mother,* and *baby and baby*. A twin's attachment to a parent is inevitably complicated by the presence of a second same-age child, and it should be assumed that a twin not only has a unique connection to his twin brother or sister but has *not* had the normal parent-child relationship.

A preliminary therapy session generally includes asking about the client's issues, his or her family history, what it was like growing up, what the relationships with his or her parents were like, how many siblings were in the family, how the client feels he or she was were parented, and so on. With a twin, a typical response to such questions might be "We weren't with our mother at all; my twin and I were just with each other. We did everything together. My mother was busy, she had other kids, we had each other, and she was sort of in the background and not a very important person." Clearly, such a response is different than a therapist would expect from a singleton client.

During the many years that I've been treating twins, clients have told me about problems and misunderstandings that arose with therapists who were unfamiliar with twin issues. They have complained that therapists who do not understand what it's like to be a twin never even bring up the twinship as a relevant topic to be discussed. And if the twin issue is the presenting problem, the therapist might say something like

"You're too close to your twin. It's an unhealthy relationship, and you've got to figure out a way to disconnect because you're too invested in your sibling." In other words, many of my clients have experienced therapists being dismissive of or insensitive to their twin-related issues. Understandably, even if a twin decides to visit a different therapist, she may worry that the new practitioner won't understand the importance of the twin connection—what it has meant, how it's been more important than her relationship to either parent, how it's been the most meaningful connection she has had, and how she doesn't know who she is apart from the twinship.

In ascertaining a client's attachment history, the therapist will come to understand that being a twin organizes and inhibits or enhances everything that person does or is. It shapes who the person is more than anything else. Unless the therapist is educated about twin issues, he or she wouldn't necessarily recognize how integral and deeply significant twinship is to the twin client, even if the client denies it. In fact, twins usually do not recognize any dysfunction related to a twin scenario until they talk about it with someone, because they perceive their interactions with and feelings about their same-age sister or brother as normal.

Therapists need to recognize that twins inhabit a unique psychological reality; they don't have the common singleton mentality that the rest of the population takes for granted. Unless therapists become oriented to the psychological environment in which twins have grown up, their twin clients will be unable to gain a valid perspective on their concerns and problems.

Twin Transference

The unconscious tendency of a client to transfer to his or her therapist feelings and attitudes associated with a parent or other significant person remains a cornerstone of psychoanalytic practice. Such feelings may be affectionate (positive transference), hostile (negative transference), or ambivalent. Given that the therapist asks a client, "How can I help you?" and says, "I want to understand you; I want to understand your problems," the therapist-client relationship often becomes a facsimile of the parent-child connection.

With a twin client, however, rather than parental transference, twin transference is more likely, with the client relating to the therapist as his twin. In twin transference, a twin client brings to the twin-therapist dyad the feelings and attitudes and expectations he feels toward his twin and their connection. Having relied on his twin for companionship, soothing, and solace, he may now look to the therapist as a twin replacement.

Since twins likely have been each other's primary attachment figure throughout their lives, they commonly crave quick and intense connections. So when a twin begins therapy, the positive transference can be immediate and deep. A therapist treating a twin should be alert to the immediacy of this connection and understand it through the lens of twin development rather than become overwhelmed and question its authenticity.

Whereas the general public assumes that twins enjoy a magical closeness, many twin pairs have never developed the skills or courage to be truly honest with each other because they are afraid of feelings and situations that may cause conflict, separation anxiety, disappointment, or competition. They need the connection to their twin and to the twinship to validate their identity, but they tend to lack access to their own inner life. Growing up as a twin very often impairs their capacity to know their authentic feelings, needs, and desires. And not having the opportunity to develop a separate self or separate identity impedes the development of real intimacy, self-awareness, and authenticity.

Given that twins' primary attachment is to each other and that they often lack access to their deepest feelings, beginning a relationship with a therapist with whom they are able to share those feelings can come as a profound surprise and awakening.

My work with Alex provides an example of how twins can be struck by their newfound ability to finally open up and share their deepest feelings. Alex entered therapy with me to understand why he had stayed in an emotionally and physically abusive relationship with his boyfriend for so long. When he broke up with the boyfriend, he looked to his twin brother to be there for him, but the brother was absolutely unavailable. He avoided and essentially abandoned Alex during a time of emotional crisis.

As he was describing the fraught situation, Alex didn't seem to have appropriate affect but rather just recited the facts. I asked him about his upbringing, and he reported that his mother had been in an abusive relationship with her husband, Alex's stepfather. The stepfather, who was a drinker, often yelled, swore, and picked fights with Alex's mother.

I asked, "Was your mother able to help you understand what was going on? Did she ask you how all this abuse and fighting affected you?" He said no. He was aware that the conflict was going on, but he didn't know how he actually felt about it.

Alex didn't have access to his feelings because his mother could not help him express or process them. For Alex and his brother, life was all about protecting their mother, being aware of the fact that she was upset, and making sure that they were good kids so as not to further upset her. They never made any fuss, never needed or wanted anything, and essentially looked after each other.

Whether or not there is extreme conflict or abuse in a family, twins who don't have a secure attachment to a parent have little access to their inner emotional life. They don't have the experience of an attentive, loving adult who asks, "Is this upsetting you? Did that make you angry?" or a parent who tells them, "I'm really sorry that Dad and I got into a fight that was scary for you." For Alex and his twin brother, the level of caregiving that they needed never took place. Instead, the two were left to take care of each other and to find solace in their own little world.

So when I became Alex's therapist, he seemed shocked when I asked if his mother ever apologized or explained what was going on. He responded, "I never thought about it." When I asked if he and his brother talked about how they felt during the years this was going on, he said that they didn't really discuss feelings. And he was never able to talk about feelings with the boyfriend he had recently broken up with either.

With Alex, the positive twin transference was reflected in the fact that he was able to take in my very pointed observations without becoming angry. At the same time, he was amazed that I could listen so intently and understand what he might be feeling about what he had been through. I shared with him that he likely had little access to his feelings because he was always attached to his twin and not to his mother, that she had never articulated what was really going on in their home and never helped him connect with his feelings. He and his brother had been on their own, together, with little emotional understanding of what they were experiencing.

Like Alex and his brother, twins very often are not the intimate friends that outsiders may assume they are, and they don't process intimate feelings with each other. So Alex couldn't even imagine talking to his brother about any of the issues we were discussing in therapy. The fact that he could be intimate with a therapist was an entirely new experience for him. His twin transference facilitated his capability to be open and honest with me in a way that he never could be with his twin. That's what is so powerful about a twin seeing a therapist who is familiar with twin psychology. The relationship represents a new experience of intimacy and authenticity to which most twins have never before had access.

Presenting Issues

Claire came to me because her twin sister's emotional dependence was jeopardizing Claire's relationship with her husband. He had recently told her that if she wanted their marriage to survive, she would have to stop seeing her sister. Claire was stunned by his demand. Having taken on the caretaker role with her sister in early childhood, she found it perfectly normal to check in with her twin several times a day and to spend time with her at least two or three times a week. Claire had no idea that she was overly involved with her sister or that her attachment to her sister was damaging her relationship with her husband. She claimed that she was surprised at how upset her husband was over her closeness to her twin sister.

Claire's struggle to save her marriage and Nick's difficulty adjusting to college away from home share a significant psychological factor: both twins were contending with core twinship issues. Nick's emotional equilibrium was thrown off when his brother was no longer there to anchor his sense of identity. And only during her therapy did Claire realize how her role as caretaker to her twin defined who she was and that relinquishing it threatened her sense of identity.

A therapist unaware of twinship issues might hear that a client's husband is annoyed by his sister-in-law's intrusive presence and not understand the wife's perspective. The therapist might also assume that a freshman's anxiety about being away from home for the first time is a relatively minor problem. But both instances involve a profound dilemma: how to let go of a lifelong identity as one half of a twinship. The therapist must understand why surrendering an identity that one has inhabited for one's entire life is exceptionally difficult and painful and that this difficulty is intrinsically related to twin attachment. Claire's and Nick's stories involve this crisis of identity, the roots of which are in their attachment histories and their ongoing attachment to their same-age siblings.

When a twin comes to therapy, the questions central to his or her problems are often, Who am I? What is my identity? The questions are not the same as those of a singleton coming in with an existential crisis, because a twin's core dilemma is, Who am I in relationship to my twin? A twin's "identity crisis" is thus fundamentally different from that of a singleton and can manifest in a range of symptomatic emotional problems.

Of course, twins are not always aware of the connection between their twinship issues and the problems that bring them to therapy. Presenting problems often include panic or anxiety attacks, depression, uncontrollable anger, feelings of abandonment, self-loathing, guilt, difficulty forming attachments, and social anxiety. The following is a compilation of the most common presenting issues for which twins seek therapy, along with the underlying factors unique to those who have grown up with a same-age sibling:

- *Panic or anxiety attacks:* Resulting from separation from one's twin after having been in a dependent attachment
- *Depression:* Resulting from the inability to acknowledge or confront feelings of rage, resentment, competitiveness, jealousy, betrayal, sadness, and so on, related to one's twinship
- *Uncontrollable anger:* Resulting from
    - Intense resentment and frustration over the other twin's dependency
    - Fairness and equality issues pertaining to one's twin
- *Feelings of abandonment:* Occurring when one's twin begins to separate and become more independent
- *Self-loathing:* Resulting from being dependent on one's twin and unable to separate
- *Guilt:* Resulting from
    - Being critical of or harsh with one's twin
    - Separating from or wanting to separate from one's twin
    - Accomplishing or attaining more than one's twin

- *Difficulty forming attachments, social anxiety:* Resulting from inexperience with relationships and the expectation of instant intimacy, given that twin closeness is "automatic"

When treating twins, a therapist must be aware of how these issues may reflect underlying circumstances and concerns that are unique to twins. The following are fundamental elements of twin psychology that will be explored in depth through case histories presented throughout the book.

- A twin who is having problems with her same-age sibling thinks of herself as part of a couple in conflict.
- Since twins are conditioned to expect effortless intimacy with their twin, they often feel deeply distraught when problems arise between them. Despair and despondency over rifts with one's twin are more common and more complicated than quarrels between nontwin siblings.
- Twins frequently feel ashamed when talking about problems they are having with their same-age sibling, as they are conditioned to believe that twinship is a gift and that twins are supposed to be emotionally in sync.
- Caretaking and being cared for by one's twin are perceived by twins as normal.
- The caretaker/cared-for twin scenario often occurs because parents of twins were insufficiently attached to each child and partially abdicated their role as caretaker in the belief that twins "naturally" take care of each other.
- Rage often underlies the anxiety and sense of annihilation that twins experience due to their being perceived as, and essentially functioning as, one half of a single entity.

- A twin may have kept his own needs in check as a child, believing that his twin's needs were greater.
- Twins often feel inauthentic because they fear that being honest with their twin might be emotionally harmful.
- A twin's perspective on her role and function in a dyad informs who she is, rather than her sense of being a self in the world.
- Twins may have little or no experience being a separate self.
- Twins often initiate therapy when they feel they have lost emotional equilibrium.
- Twins need a trusted outsider to give them perspective about their twinship. They need to know that a therapist is knowledgeable about twinship issues and how to overcome them.

CHAPTER 2

Excessive Interdependence

"I'm not worried about myself," Andy told me in our first session, "I'm worried about Brian. I'm worried that he's so depressed, and nothing I do makes any difference. I've worked so hard to try to help him in every conceivable way. I've tried everything I can think of and now I'm out of options and I'm just so angry—really angry—and I don't know what to do at this point. Neither of us can get anything done or even function anymore, and—"

Brian had said nothing up to now. He sat on the floor, the hood of his sweatshirt pulled over his head. At fifty-one, he appeared younger than his identical twin, Andy, but he was clearly withdrawn and depressed. In fact, both brothers were on antidepressants. As Andy spoke, his rapid-fire sentences leaving little space for either me or Brian to get a word in, Brian kept his head down. Finally breaking into Andy's monologue, Brian uttered his one-liner: "I just want to move out and be on my own."

"We both do," Andy fired back. "We both want to move. We both want to be on our own. We both know that this is the worst possible situation for us to be in. We can't stand each other, but we can't go off on our own now. We just can't do it now because of our current economic situation."

Andy and Brian had been living together for fifteen years, beginning in their midthirties, and the "current" economic situation to which

Andy referred had actually persisted for nearly that entire period. But the reasons these middle-aged twin brothers were still living together extended beyond their financial troubles. The psychological issues that kept them from leading satisfying, independent lives had been developing over decades.

Andy had found my book *The Same but Different* on the internet. Eager to talk to a twin specialist, he set up the first session with me for both him and his brother. Both agreed, however, that they wanted to see separate therapists. So after that initial session, I saw Andy on his own and referred Brian to a colleague. Over the course of his therapy, Andy and I explored the path that had led him to the impasse with his brother, the obstacles that impeded his progress, and the changes that might propel his way forward.

Inadequate Parental Validation and Mirroring

As Andy described his childhood, he emphasized that the brothers managed to keep things "even-steven" by excelling in their own ways. In middle school, Brian made the baseball team, and Andy was in the band. In high school, Andy enjoyed being on the debate team, and Brian took photographs for the school paper. Andy took pride in his ability to speak intelligently and logically in front of an audience, which he claimed was honed around the dinner table at home, where he tried his best to impress his parents with what he had read or learned in school. Having a voice at the table—being able to contribute to his parents' conversation and being recognized for having something smart to say—was very important to him.

While Andy felt that throughout their youth he and Brian balanced each other out so that neither of them outshined the other, he also believed that no one in his family truly saw him, appreciated him, or gave him credit for his accomplishments. This belief continued to plague him, which accounted for much of his anger and resentment toward not only his parents but Brian as well. At the same time, Brian was the only person with whom Andy had an ongoing relationship—however fraught and adversarial it had become. Andy had no close friends and had never had an intimate relationship that lasted longer than a few weeks.

As we began to explore his childhood, Andy often repeated that when he and Brian were very young, they were "the apple of our mother's eye. She admired and loved us," he said. "But once we were no longer good little boys and became confrontational and argumentative, she turned on us. She became angry and disappointed, and that was the beginning of the end of our relationship with our mom." As for their father, he was not very involved with them, other than occasionally giving attention to the boys' remarks during dinner conversations, according to Andy.

The essential role of a parent is to provide validation, mirroring, and encouragement to his or her child, which ideally leads to the development of self-esteem that the young person can then take out into the world. Since Andy and Brian didn't receive focused, validating attention from either parent, they turned to each other for a semblance of mutual caretaking. Being psychologically unequipped to nurture each other, unable to mirror or validate each other, Andy and Brian instead formed a symbiotic relationship common to many twins. They were continually aware of how the other brother was feeling and responding and vigilant as to how their own decisions and behavior were affecting their twin. Every activity they engaged in, every opinion they voiced, was perceived in terms of their dyadic relationship. Since they had no core self outside the twinship, every attitude and every action was about what effect it would have on their brother. And every ability or accomplishment was evaluated with regard to how it measured up against the other brother's achievements.

E. D. Joseph and J. H. Tabor, in an article appearing in the *Psychoanalytic Study of the Child,* refer to what they call the twinning reaction, defined as "(1) mutual interidentification and (2) part fusion of the self-representation and the object representation of the other member of the [twin] pair."[1] Elizabeth Stewart summarizes the twinning reaction as "mutual interdependence and failure completely to differentiate one's self from the other."[2]

It became apparent in my sessions with Andy that the brothers' excessive interdependence had led to confusion of self and other. Andy was unable to articulate whatever feeling he was experiencing or whatever problem he was having in his life without referencing Brian. He couldn't perceive any situation or emotion as an individual; everything he felt or experienced was either in contrast to, in support of, or somehow in relationship to his twin brother. But at this point in their middle-aged lives, the interdependent connection was paralyzing both of them. How had these fifty-one-year-old twins reached the point where they made each other so miserable that they couldn't function, where they desperately wanted to separate from each other but couldn't see a way out?

Banking on Twin Synergy

After getting along fairly well in high school by adhering to their unspoken "even-steven" arrangement, Andy and Brian attended the same college. They each did fairly well scholastically and took part in separate activities. Brian had a girlfriend for a while, which Andy referred to as "a disaster." According to Andy, the young woman was "crazy," and as he watched Brian go through a very traumatic situation, Andy became aware that getting involved with the wrong woman could be dangerous. Brian's college romance also alienated Andy because Brian was no longer available to spend time with him. Andy mentioned that he saw a college counselor to talk about his own lack of success with women but stopped going after a few unproductive sessions.

After college, Brian moved away and got a job working for a small graphic design company and Andy got an entry-level public relations job back home. He and Andy checked in with each other at least two or three times a week, enjoying their friendly chats on the phone. Over the next decade and a half, neither brother had made much progress in his career. As they approached the age of thirty-five, both were feeling unfulfilled and at loose ends. Brian had recently broken up with a girlfriend and was looking to make a change. So he and Andy decided to borrow money from their parents, move in together, and start an online business. It seemed like the perfect time to reconnect and take advantage of their twin synergy.

Andy said he had been convinced that being twins in business together would be an ideal situation: "We are so aware of how the other guy thinks and operates—and we just get each other. I have my strengths; Brian has his. We wouldn't have to put up with the crap we had to put up with in our previous jobs. . . . We just figured there was no way we could fail."

They had come up with a solution to the hard times and marginal existence they had endured for far too long: live, create, and succeed together. At thirtysomething, they shared a fantasy—an idealized sense that merging their lives would mean they would be more successful as a team than either had been on his own.

Andy and Brian bought into the twin mystique. Although they had never before collaborated on a project or been involved in a start-up, they believed they would be so in sync that, despite their lack of experience, they could overcome the odds and create a profitable enterprise. They were banking on twin synergy to rescue them from their lackluster lives—and "save the day," as Andy described it.

Fairly soon after they moved in together and began working on developing their business, Andy and Brian realized that they were unable to collaborate. They were constantly fighting, unable to discuss their differences in a civilized manner, unable to compromise, and thus unable to get anything accomplished. The issue that most threatened their partnership is one that plagues excessively interdependent twins: their fused identity meant that Andy was unable to separate Brian's alleged shortcomings from his own sense of self. He took it personally when Brian didn't go about things in the precise way Andy advised. Andy told me, "We can't work together or get anything done. Brian hates me, he thinks I'm critical and overbearing, but he doesn't understand how I'm trying to help him." For Andy, "trying to help" Brian meant telling him specifically how various tasks should be accomplished.

Andy was constantly critical of Brian's graphic design concepts and communication style. When they lost a major project, Brian blamed Andy's abrasive manner with the potential client. The fact that the brothers were at odds was obvious to their business contacts and reflected poorly on their fledgling enterprise. The business was going nowhere, funding was being depleted, and the brothers' personal relationship was deteriorating. Their unrealistic expectation of miraculously succeeding in a flash of twin dynamism descended into ongoing acrimony between the brothers.

Andy said that he and Brian went through periods of not talking to each other for days because if they talked, they would automatically clash. One would try to prove his point, the other would counter, and the exchange would escalate into an untenable situation. Often, Andy would "go crazy" trying to make himself understood, only to then feel guilty when Brian became upset and withdrew, refusing to talk to him. Or Brian would roll his eyes and become "quietly nasty," which made Andy furious. They could not have a conversation about anything where they could agree to disagree. Locked in a stalemate day in and day out, either they were bickering back and forth and not getting anywhere, or they were not talking at all, each in his own room, staying out of the other's way. Andy was convinced that both of them had been engaged in a strategy of baiting one another and being baited, and for that reason,

Andy was constantly vigilant—on guard to protect himself from what he perceived as Brian's subtle yet intentional emotional assaults.

Quarreling Means Feeling Separate

A lot of my work with Andy involved helping him understand his heightened responses to disagreements with Brian—and what he could do to manage himself. Instead of trying to manage Brian or even understand Brian, Andy had to figure out a way to take care of himself so that he wasn't devastated by differences of opinion with Brian to the point where he couldn't focus on his work. Andy told me that his main goal in therapy was to overcome his emotional paralysis and be able to get his work done.

We discussed that to achieve that goal, Andy had to find a way to not feel upset or guilty about a perceived conflict with Brian and to not be impinged upon by Brian's moods and passive-aggressive behavior. Andy's challenge was that any hint of a fight or disagreement with Brian—even an unpleasant look on Brian's face or anything else that made Andy feel that Brian was angry or upset with him—would have the capacity to throw Andy into a tailspin to such an extent that on really bad days he couldn't get out of bed.

I tried to help Andy understand why he felt like this. Not having received adequate mirroring and validation from his parents, he had turned to Brian—not an unusual circumstance in twin relationships. But over the years his unacknowledged reliance on the twinship for his sense of identity had left Andy with little capacity to feel that he had a self apart from his connection to Brian. Their fused identity led Andy to believe (consciously or unconsciously) that he and his brother had to be in strict agreement. The minute one of them veered from that brotherly solidarity, the resulting imbalance was terrifying for Andy. So while Andy needed the conflict with his brother to have some sense of being a separate person, arguing with Brian, and thereby breaking the idealized "unbreakable bond," was profoundly traumatic. I helped Andy recognize that although their ongoing friction had become a constant source of irritation, his opposition to Brian was an unconscious attempt to separate from him.

As Stewart points out in her summation of Joseph and Tabor's concept of the twinning reaction,

> This twinning reaction is opposed by a drive toward separation and individuation: "It is the interplay between the 'twinning reaction' and the striving for individuation that forms the matrix for the behavior of twins and for understanding the nature of the twinship."[3]

Andy's animosity toward Brian was his "drive toward separation and individuation" in that his angry reactions provided him with a semblance of self. He both feared and needed conflict with Brian.

Fear of conflict had also been a hallmark of Andy's workplace relationships prior to moving in with Brian in their thirties. He recalled that he couldn't tolerate any differences of opinion between himself and his coworkers because he couldn't control himself when disagreements occurred. He maintained a standoffish demeanor because he feared that if he and a colleague disagreed, he would lose his composure. Andy had formed no intimate connections with anyone because such relationships would cause him to feel threatened and criticized, which would then trigger him to lose control and lash out. He said he had to be really careful because he knew on some level that his trigger points were obvious.

Unable to connect with friends or colleagues or a romantic partner, Andy's sole access to companionship was with Brian. Brian was also the only person whom Andy could safely live with because if Andy got triggered by conflicts or disagreements, he felt that everything would ultimately be okay between him and his brother. At least that's what he initially thought when the two moved in together. But after years of bickering, hurt feelings, and stalemate, neither brother was okay. If Brian was depressed, Andy would get depressed. If Brian didn't go along with a business decision, Andy felt hurt and angry—and then guilty for feeling angry.

Andy and I talked about how twins often take on the feelings of their same-age sibling and then become overwhelmed, confused, and paralyzed by doing so. They feel their own feelings but simultaneously those of their twin as well, and the merging of the two is overwhelming. Andy felt overwhelmed all the time, partly because he genuinely cared about Brian and, as his twin, couldn't help taking on Brian's feelings, but also because "worrying about" and quarreling with Brian was a way for Andy to avoid dealing with his own frailties and vulnerabilities.

Unhappy Couples

Andy and Brian are in some ways similar to couples who are unhappy in their marriage, who drive each other crazy but would rather not live alone, who would rather maintain the security of companionship even if their companion is far from desirable. The known quantity of their spouse is preferable to the unknown of striking out on their own.

Unhappily married couples and unhappy twins who remain together (like Andy and Brian) have a key attribute in common: they are stuck in the comfort-discomfort of their dyadic roles with little momentum toward change. Of course the difference between a married couple and a twin couple is that twins don't choose each other; they are born into the dyad. Nonetheless, just as a newly married couple hopes for a successful marriage, Andy and Brian hoped for a successful career together, living and working in tandem. They imagined that they would join forces, enjoy a well-functioning collaborative relationship, and create a thriving business. But Andy and Brian's relationship carries with it uniquely problematic baggage. Their early interdependence developed as a consequence of inadequate parental nurturing, they became each other's insufficient surrogate guardian, and their ongoing interdependence resulted in their inability to develop separate selves.

Andy and Brian have remained as roommates and business partners. They contend that, although they are both dissatisfied with their living and work situation, they have to stay together for economic reasons. After Andy's year and a half in therapy, his living arrangement has not changed, but his perspective and behavior have.

Becoming Less Emotionally Invested in One's Twin

When Andy started therapy with me, he was so overly sensitized to Brian's responses and feelings and so unable to handle them that he defended himself against all feelings—anger, sadness, hurt, confusion. He did this by implicitly demanding of Brian, "Don't argue with me, don't get upset with me, don't roll your eyes, don't say I'm not being a wonderful person. Just appreciate everything I'm doing and see that everything I'm doing is for you. If you just appreciate me and love me and see the sacrifices I'm making for you, you'll be fine and I will feel good about myself."

Andy couldn't handle the fact that Brian would not go along with these demands. He was so fragile and vulnerable that he was unable to accept Brian's perspective. Andy's core issue was that he was forever trying to incorporate two separate people into his singular sense of self. If Brian didn't mirror his opinions, Andy felt dismissed, misunderstood, and rejected because for twins whose connection is excessively interdependent, there is no self without the other.

In one of our sessions, I related an incident that had occurred between my twin sister and me. It involved our profound disagreement about what was or wasn't appropriate at a family wedding we had recently attended. I tried to convey to Andy that you can have a conversation with your twin and feel that his perspective makes absolutely no sense to you, but you can still agree to disagree. While that may sound simple enough, Andy didn't understand what it meant to have a subjective perspective. For him, an opinion was always about facts. In his view, when Brian argued with him, it meant he was not accepting the facts. If Brian would just correctly interpret the facts, he would have no choice but to agree with Andy. The notion of acknowledging the validity of another person's viewpoint was completely foreign to Andy. And that came from the twinship. Twins who are excessively interdependent feel that they must consistently be on the same page; otherwise, an unnatural and dangerous imbalance exists. Andy struggled to understand his resistance to the concepts I offered.

But he was motivated to change. He wanted to be in therapy, he wanted to understand himself, and he wanted to feel better. Once we explored why he was unable to tolerate Brian's perspective—out of an ongoing need to be in sync with his brother, which had its roots in his inadequate parenting and excessive interdependence with Brian—Andy was incredibly open and authentic in our subsequent sessions. He said, "I know how sensitive I am. I can't stand anyone getting angry at me. I fall apart if someone's angry or sad. If someone is having too many feelings, I immediately change the subject. But I don't want to be this way."

Andy came to understand that he could work at feeling less guilty about Brian's situation, less responsible, and less involved. Being less invested in Brian's well-being would give Andy a sense of his own independence so that he would not be triggered by Brian's responses and behavior. Andy could then feel more entitled to be on his own emotionally, to move forward, and to accomplish what he wanted to do without Brian's approval. And that would make him feel a lot better.

After much effort, Andy made progress in the business that the brothers had started years before. He had to teach himself a number of new skills, which was indeed challenging. But he made a major decision: rather than become embroiled in disagreements that would trigger his anger and vulnerability, he negotiated with Brian to take on certain responsibilities himself. Accepting that he would not involve Brian in particular aspects of the business was a major developmental step for Andy. He would no longer be fearful of Brian's reactions, how Brian was going to feel, or how Brian might treat him. That decision represented a leap forward.

No longer stymied by worries or concerns about Brian's every emotional response, Andy began to experience an authentic separateness. Taking this action—consciously excluding Brian, knowing that it might cause friction and bad feelings but also knowing that he could handle those feelings without becoming devastated—was a triumph for Andy: "I feel justified in making this change. I'm going to have to handle the bad feelings, but I know I have to do this because otherwise the work will never get done. I'm making an independent decision on my own, and going forward with it."

For Andy, it was more than just a business decision; it represented a key step toward separation and individuation.

A Twin's Need for Therapeutic Validation

The process that emerged in my sessions with Andy involved his talking nearly incessantly for the entire hour. At times it was difficult for me to be patient with the repetition of what he chose to talk about; however, I was careful not to interfere with his need for an understanding, validating listener. I was aware of his fragile, defensive demeanor, as he would often repeat statements such as "I'm sensitive," "I'm thin-skinned," "I can't stand criticism," and "I don't like it when anyone is upset with me." I think his fear of being criticized, misunderstood, or overwhelmed was why Andy talked nonstop during our sessions; it was his way of defending against my interjecting my opinions, being critical, or being invasive.

In his relationship with Brian, if Andy felt that he was not completely understood or that Brian was criticizing him in any way, it was a blow to Andy's fragile sense of self. So I surmise that's why he never wanted me to say very much in our sessions. My role was to be patient, careful, attentive, and caring—while Andy expressed all his ambivalent feelings. I had to be very careful about how and when I said something. As Andy spoke unremittingly, he required that I just be quiet, gentle, and loving and not tread upon him—to simply understand him. And that's what I did.

I believe my behavior during our sessions was beneficial because increasingly, Andy came to trust me and was able to dig deeper into why he was so defensive. He became very open in saying "I'm so sensitive, I can't handle criticism. I don't like to be with other people because I get triggered so easily. I don't really want to have that many attachments because I find them unsafe."

When Andy ended therapy, he was able to strike out on his own to a limited degree by not factoring in Brian's expected responses or input, and that was a major step. However, his steadfast reluctance to get involved with anyone other than Brian persisted. His interdependence with Brian meant that Andy was unable to comfortably forge attachments with anyone else. In fact, our therapeutic process revealed that he couldn't tolerate being connected to me unless I consistently and predictably validated his perspectives and feelings. He kept me at arm's length because our attachment—as productive as it had been—was still overwhelming to him if I reflected a dissenting point of view or subjective perspective that did not mirror his thoughts or emotions.

Although interdependent twins lack a sense of self outside the dyad, each has unique therapeutic needs. For example, whereas my reliable validation of Andy was key to his therapy, Brian may not have required such exquisite attunement. In the following case study, the client, Owen, needed a therapist who could help him understand the roots of his shame and effectively overcome his feelings of abandonment.

Confronting Abandonment

Owen's mother called me because she was worried about her son. Thirty-one years old and an identical twin, Owen was depressed and had withdrawn from his normal activities, no longer the outgoing young man everyone loved. The mother assumed that her son's depression stemmed from the fact that about six months earlier, his twin brother, Oliver, had moved to the city—about fifty miles from the small town where Owen and his mom lived—to be with his boyfriend.

During my phone consultation with Owen and Oliver's mother, she provided some general background information. The brothers had always been close. Growing up, they enjoyed being together and were each other's "best buddy." They excelled on sports teams together, had the same circle of friends, and were well liked by everyone. In high school, Oliver came out as gay, which wasn't a big deal for either Owen or the boys' parents. After attending the same community college, the brothers decided to capitalize on their physical abilities and got jobs coteaching spin classes and aerobic workout classes at an upscale fitness club. The two enjoyed their jobs so much and had such a great following among the gym members that they toyed with the idea of opening their own gym. They got as far as consulting with a local bank's loan officer. But when Oliver decided to move to the city, those plans fell by the wayside.

Owen quit his job at the gym soon after his brother left, telling his mom that going there made him too sad because it reminded him of his days with Oliver. He took some time off and traveled for a few months. When he returned, he got another job but essentially cut himself off from his friends and the activities he used to enjoy. Prior to Oliver's move, the brothers had shared an apartment. Now Owen was living with his mother again. His mom said, "I've never seen Owen so despondent, and I really don't know what to do. Oliver is concerned about him, too, and agreed with me that I should contact you. In fact, he would be happy to be in on the therapy."

I thought seeing the brothers together would be a good idea so that I could gain a clearer sense of their relationship and how it might be impacting Owen's current state of mind. Owen consented to travel to meet twice a month for our sessions, and Oliver lived not far from my office.

During our first session, Owen told me that he wasn't really depressed, as his mother had conveyed to me. "I'm just having a hard time right now with my new job," he said. "It's basically an office job and not what I want to be doing."

Oliver wondered why Owen hadn't gone back to his job at the gym. "They love you there, bro," he said. Owen said he'd lost interest in it. Oliver turned and gave me a meaningful look. "We were a real force at that gym," he told me. "Everyone knew us as 'the Os'—Owen and Oliver. Right, Owen?"

"Yeah, I guess," Owen said.

I asked Owen how he had been affected by Oliver's move. He was silent for a few moments and then said, "I'm happy for him. I think it was a great move . . . and Jay's a great guy."

The two talked about a recent weekend visit Owen had made to the city. Oliver's boyfriend, Jay, was very welcoming. He made a fantastic dinner, and the three of them had a good time playing volleyball with some friends at the beach. It was clear to me that Owen was trying his best to put a good face on the changes that had occurred in the brothers' lives. "He and Jay have a great apartment," he said, after which Oliver asked him how long he was planning to live with their mom and whether he was looking for a roommate. Owen confessed that he had no plans to move and no idea whom to live with.

In the next session, I asked the brothers to talk about their relationship over the years. Oliver mentioned how fun-loving and outgoing they were as kids, teenagers, and college students. They both said that they never fought and were not competitive as children. "Our parents appreciated the fact that we got along so well and were each other's best friend," Oliver said. "It meant they didn't have to worry about us fighting with each other like most brothers. We just had fun together."

Owen remembered that there was another set of twins in middle school and that they hated each other. "I could never understand that," he said.

Since they lived in a small town, the two couldn't go anywhere alone without being asked, "Where's your other half?" Neither of them minded the focus on their being twins; in fact, they said they enjoyed it. While Oliver was very open as he relayed his feelings about how much he valued their relationship, Owen was guarded. It was as if it hurt too much to talk about such a close connection that they no longer shared.

As the brothers spoke, I could see that as adults, they had basically lived their lives as an enmeshed couple. Not only had they worked at the same fitness club, but they got up every morning and worked out together, had lunch together, hung out with the same friends, and stayed out late partying together.

I knew that my objective was to help Owen figure out what his feelings were about his separation from Oliver so that he could articulate and talk about them. I also could see that not only was Owen sad and depressed, he was also angry at his brother for abandoning him and for ruining the plans they had made to open their own gym. But it wasn't easy for Owen to open up about feeling abandoned and distraught. To do so would provoke a tremendous amount of shame.

Feeling ashamed for being upset over the loss of companionship with one's twin is common for adult same-age siblings, especially those whose identities have become essentially merged, as Owen's and Oliver's had been. Twins often consider themselves "not normal" for feeling distraught about separating from their sibling. After all, for singleton siblings, this would not normally be an issue. Although admitting to being upset when a romantic partner moves away is socially acceptable, becoming distressed when your twin moves out of town is humiliating, which is why harboring such embarrassing feelings is shameful. It is especially shameful given that adult twins feel they should be mature enough to accept separation from their same-age sibling. Missing your brother when you're five or ten years old is one thing, but when you're thirty-one, it is considered by nontwins to be weird. So for twins to feel such a sense of loss makes *them* feel weird—and ashamed—as well.

A therapist who is unfamiliar with twinship issues might not understand how shame plays a role in a client's unwillingness to acknowledge his or her feelings, and in Owen's case, it was a major factor. I could tell that Owen's sense of shame was preventing him from articulating his sadness, distress, anger, and disappointment over Oliver's moving away to be with his boyfriend. In a very real sense, Oliver had chosen his lover over Owen. But Owen didn't yet feel ready to acknowledge—much less articulate—his feelings of abandonment.

In our next session, I began by asking Owen if he had been at all upset when he found out that Oliver was moving. "No, not really," he said.

Oliver waited a moment and then told his brother that he felt guilty about choosing to move, that it really was a loyalty conflict for him: staying and starting a business with his brother or moving out of town to be with the guy he was in love with. He said it put him in a terrible bind, but he had to follow his heart and be with his lover. "I completely understand how you feel, though," Oliver said. "If the situation were turned around, I would feel upset and angry, too." Oliver was more open, more forthcoming with his feelings—because clearly he felt less conflicted. He had made the choice to separate from Owen, even though he felt bad to be causing his brother such pain.

Owen repeated that he was happy for Oliver. Still harboring tremendous shame about feeling abandoned, he couldn't allow himself to admit his feelings. So he defended against the shame by saying that he was not really upset.

I decided to interject and addressed Owen: "There were really three major changes to your relationship in the last six months. Not only did Oliver find a boyfriend, but he decided not to go through with the plan to open a gym together and moved out of town as well. How did you feel about those changes, Owen?"

Owen said nothing at first; then he uttered quietly that he honestly just wanted Oliver to be happy. Oliver put his arm around Owen, and we agreed to pick up with the brothers' separation in our next session.

The following week, Oliver turned to Owen and began the session: "I just want to say you must have really felt awful when I decided to move and to abandon our plans to open a gym. I know I would have fallen apart if it had been me. I'm really sorry, Owen. I didn't mean to hurt you, but I needed to make a selfish decision to be with my boyfriend. I know I must have really hurt you . . . and I'm so sorry."

Owen began to cry. He was finally able to say, "Yeah, you left me . . . and I felt at a loss. I'm glad you're happy, and I know you love Jay, but what am I supposed to do?"

Oliver went over to Owen and gave him a hug. Somewhat awkwardly, Owen accepted it.

Validating Feelings, Overcoming Shame

When a client in a therapy session hears a heartfelt statement coming directly from the person who has hurt him or her, it has a much greater impact than if the therapist were to say, for example: "I know your brother must have really hurt you" or "I know you must feel really abandoned by your brother." When Oliver communicated to Owen that he took responsibility for causing him pain, Owen's feelings of abandonment were validated. Of course, Owen still felt depressed and abandoned, but now he could openly acknowledge why he was so sad and miserable, without feeling as ashamed of those feelings.

Shame is the most pernicious feeling of all—for any of us. So when one person validates another's potentially shameful feelings, those feelings are no longer something to be ashamed of. Once Oliver validated Owen's feelings, enabling him to let go of the shame, Owen was able to get to the depression and the anger. Knowing that his feelings were understandable and normal lifted him out of a shame-based place and allowed him to feel and express the sadness and disappointment caused by the brothers' separation.

In the next session, Owen began seeing me on his own. He referred to having cried in the last session with Oliver and said that he had never before felt out of control—and that the feelings of loneliness and disconnection that made him cry and feel anxious were his first experience in thirty-one years of actually feeling anything other than a kind of automatic togetherness with his brother. He had had relationships with girlfriends over the years but nothing lasting. "My last girlfriend told me she couldn't read me," he said, "and I was never really sure what she meant." He mentioned that not until a year after he had broken up with her did he realize he had loved her.

I suggested that perhaps his relationship difficulties were at least in part due to his inability to be in touch with his feelings and that this could be related to how easy or "automatic" the twinship relationship was. Any connection other than the one with his brother could be intimidating.

As Owen worked through his painful feelings about separating from Oliver, I helped him begin to figure out who he was as an individual self, apart from his brother. I asked him to consider what he really wanted to do with his life and whether he wanted to pursue the plans he had initially made with Oliver: Did he still want to open a gym? Were there personal strengths and skills that he now wanted to employ and develop? Had developing any of these strengths been put on hold because of his emotional interdependence with Oliver?

While he acknowledged that he still wanted to use his physical skills as he had at the gym, Owen identified an untapped quality that might benefit him as he thought about a potential new career: his approachability and friendliness. He told me that people always seemed to gravitate toward him without his having to put on an act. He thought that, rather than owning a gym, maybe he could be a personal trainer, thereby employing the social skills that he had always taken for granted and underutilized.

We talked about how the one-on-one aspect of being a personal trainer would be a positive challenge. Throughout his life, Owen's sole one-on-one connection had been with his brother. The two had always been popular, outgoing, and well liked—but in the context of their being a duo. Now he would have the opportunity to establish one-on-one professional relationships with clients who hired him as their fitness trainer. As a separate person engaging with others in this way, he would have a new perspective on himself.

Thinking about how he would function in the world without his twin involved developmental steps that Owen had never had to tackle before. Our therapy sessions were part of that process in that he had to develop a new skill: sharing his feelings with another person. Since his emotional communication and interactions with Oliver had essentially been nonverbal and "automatic," as Owen put it, he had never had to articulate how he felt. While our time together had yielded emotional insights, Owen still struggled when talking about his feelings. Still, he was now able to access those feelings and use them to help guide his future decisions.

Benefits of Twin Couples Therapy

The fact that initially Owen and Oliver came to therapy together was very beneficial. Oliver's empathic resonance with Owen's feelings of sadness, anger, and abandonment helped Owen let go of his shame; it also enabled both young men to get to know each other in a way neither had previously experienced.

Very often when twin couples come to therapy, they don't really know who the other one is except in relationship to the twinship. So they need help in figuring out Who is this other person whom I've known all my life but don't really know? Accustomed to viewing their twin through the lens of growing up together—inhabiting the same space, being a partner and competitor, having a shared identity—they often have no clue as to who this person is as an individual adult.

Twins are often unaware of their same-age sibling's deeper motives, emotions, sensitivities, and intentions. They may never have had a chance to discover each other's authentic differences—those that go beyond the superficial labels used to differentiate twins: *the outgoing one, the studious one, the rebel*. Because their childhood was shared and dyadically organized, adult twins may not really know each other as separate people, apart from their twinship identity. Being seen together in therapy provides an opportunity for this interpersonal discovery to happen.

Although Owen's presenting problem was depression, I was grateful to have seen the brothers together initially. Oliver's ability to acknowledge his feelings and validate Owen's helped the therapeutic process immeasurably. Seeing the brothers together also allowed me to witness their close connection firsthand and to understand more clearly how challenging it would be for Owen to separate from Oliver.

In *Alone in the Mirror: Twins in Therapy*, author Barbara Klein notes the importance of respecting the twin attachment when seeing twins together in therapy:

> Being even-handed and respecting the twin attachment, which to the outsider may seem dysfunctional, is the first and most important goal. In my experience, not taking sides is very difficult because one twin will appear stronger and more effective at solving problems. The other member of the pair may be more comfortable with denial. The therapist must use her best listening skills and compassion, being careful to avoid making a judgment of one twin as more competent and the other as less able to work through their issues.[4]

By working through his feelings of being abandoned and lost without his brother, Owen began to take steps to comfortably separate from

Oliver. The two still share a loving, close connection. But what was once an excessive interdependence—in which they shared the same workplace, social life, and home base—has given way to two individual lives. Oliver enjoys his independence and romantic relationship, and Owen feels increasingly confident that he has the tools to develop a separate self.

CHAPTER 3

Good Twin/Bad Twin

Holly was not doing well. I had been seeing her for several months as she continued to struggle with intense social anxiety and the anger and self-loathing that accompanied it. During one session, she told me how miserable she had been at a party she had attended over the weekend: "I was so humiliated. I went to this party with my friend Ruthie and I just wanted to disappear. Everyone but me was having a great time. Ruthie left me on my own and was out there dancing with the rest of them, and I just can't do that. I was dying to leave, but Ruthie was obviously having fun and couldn't have cared less about me. I felt trapped and self-conscious and really pissed off. At Ruthie . . . but also at myself. Why am I like this?"

An identical twin, twenty-five-year-old Holly had a pattern of trying to make friends but feeling demeaned and angry when those friendships didn't work out. Her twin sister, Samantha, on the other hand, seemed to attract both girlfriends and boyfriends without even trying. "Even when Sam treats people like she doesn't care if they're her friend or not," said Holly, "everyone wants to be around her because she's superconfident and full of herself. And I guess people think she's fun to be around."

Holly's feelings of inferiority and inadequacy, as well as her inability to establish lasting friendships, can be traced to her relationship with Samantha. As very often occurs in a twinship, early in their lives the girls had taken on the roles of good twin and bad twin. More accurately, those roles had been unconsciously assigned to them by their parents.

In consulting with Holly's mother, I learned that as an infant, Holly had been more prone to fussing and crying jags; Samantha generally had been a more easygoing baby. The mom obviously loved them both and wanted the best for them, but she likely had an unacknowledged preference for Samantha as a child and thus a closer attachment to her. Very often in a twinship, the less challenging child becomes more closely attached to the parent, which results in the other twin feeling left out and attaching instead to his or her twin. In this particular triadic configuration, the twin to whom the parent is attached is unconsciously perceived as good, and the one who feels left out and attaches more closely to his or her twin is unconsciously perceived as bad. Even so, the "good twin" suffers negative consequences for being the preferred child. He or she not only experiences feelings of guilt for being related to as the good one but also is assigned the role of caretaker to the "bad twin."

Barbara Klein offers these insights on parental attachment as it relates to the good/bad twin split:

> The parent has an individualized and judgmental attachment to each twin based on an assumption that one child is the opposite of the other, for example, good/bad, strong/weak. Each twin gradually internalizes and adopts parental judgments about his own identity and their parents' perceptions of the twins' identity. Because the initial twin attachment is based on comfort and sharing, twins learning about their parents' judgments develop ambivalence toward each other as they grow.[1]

Samantha was definitely identified as the good twin. Outwardly happy, engaged, and socially successful, she did better in school than Holly and had fewer behavioral problems. Holly was rebellious, got in trouble with teachers, told people off when her feelings were hurt, which was frequently, and infringed on Sam by leaning on her in social situations.

Holly resented feeling "less than" Samantha and hated being socially and emotionally dependent on her sister. And Samantha hated bearing the ongoing burden of her sister's dependence. The sisters fought constantly. Their mom felt sorry for Holly and thus rarely reprimanded her for her bad behavior. Buying into Holly's sense of being unfairly victimized, the mom failed to properly guide her in coping with challenges. She hoped that when the sisters went away to separate colleges, Holly would be free to find her own way and to forget the childhood comparisons to her more carefree, successful sister.

Problem Child versus Successful Child

Unfortunately, the die had been cast. Holly continued to behave according to her designated role as the troubled bad twin. Having lacked healthy parenting, she had not developed the capacity to regulate herself in challenging situations. In college, where she could no longer count on Samantha to help her navigate social environments, Holly felt awkward and was unreasonably sensitive. Fearful of being rejected, she often used the excuse of having been treated poorly to abruptly reject a prospective friend early in the relationship. Unsure of herself in the unfamiliar situation of being on her own, she felt increasingly victimized.

Because she had been infantilized by her parents, Holly had never learned to take responsibility for herself or her actions. Beginning in high school and throughout college, when Samantha was unwilling or unavailable to be Holly's caretaker, the girls' parents tried to rescue Holly by letting her get away with being irresponsible. They continued to go along with the notion that Holly was a victim of her sister's and other people's lack of empathy. But their well-meaning overprotection of their "problem child" only exacerbated Holly's emotional handicaps.

Holly's ongoing resentment of Samantha's successes fueled her desperation as well as her belief that her sister should take care of her. But her neediness was humiliating, so she masked it with aggressive acting out. Since early childhood, Holly had inhabited her role as the bad twin, and that persona organized who she was as a young adult.

After graduating from college and entering the workforce, Holly repeatedly became upset with people who she felt were unfairly critical at work. In her few years as an employee, she had already quit several jobs due to her inability to stay the course when interpersonal difficulties arose. "I just can't put up with people treating me that way," she told me more than a few times when reporting that she was no longer employed at a job she had recently taken.

Sadly, Holly benefited from being the identified problem child—in contrast to her sister's position as the successful one. The unspoken twin designations enabled Holly to insist on what she would and would not do, what she wanted and didn't want. At the same time, the comparisons between her and Samantha—in her own mind and in the minds of her family and friends—had made Holly excessively sensitive and vulnerable. She had internalized the successful-child/problem-child comparison, which she then defended against by feeling that she was smarter than other people. As an employee, this translated into her not following certain protocols or taking orders from anyone. In our sessions, she insisted that she had a hard time finding the right job because, as she put it, "I won't be belittled or criticized by someone who doesn't respect me!"

Feeling less than Samantha throughout their childhood, hostile toward her yet dependent on her, and bolstered in her victimhood by her parents' overprotection, Holly is internally organized as a fragile, insecure, self-conscious girl who is hurt and intimidated and rejected by everyone. She deals with this ongoing emotional onslaught by becoming haughty, critical, and judgmental toward everyone around her. In this way she attempts to protect herself from the overwhelming feelings she is trying not to feel.

Parents of twins may have difficulty avoiding the common inclination to compare their same-age children. Unfortunately, Holly and Samantha's perceived bad/good dichotomy clearly played a part in their parents' treatment of the girls. The parents enabled Holly to feel victimized by allowing their guilt about her being less than Samantha to give rise to their overprotection and lack of guidance. Certainly Holly struggled more than her sister, both academically and socially, but if the girls had been singletons, would their parents have given Holly a pass when it came to her bad behavior and hurt feelings? And if she hadn't received such a pass, might Holly have developed the inner strength to deal with what life threw her way? While parents of nontwin siblings may compare their children's personalities and strengths, and while the children's awareness of such comparisons can affect their sense of self-worth, parental comparisons have a much greater emotional impact on twins.

Another reason Holly seemed stuck in the role of the bad twin or problem child was related to a normal desire to distinguish herself from her same-age sibling. Holly's acting out, getting into trouble, and battling with her sister over the years were obvious ways for her to establish her separateness from Samantha. Twins commonly vent their frustration over constantly being compared to each other by outwardly demonstrating how different they are from their twin and how intensely they oppose their twin sister or brother. In fact, Holly often complained to me that she hated feeling that she was always being compared to Samantha. "Everyone wants me to be more like her, like she sets the standard or something," she said. As much as Holly needed and depended on Samantha, she yearned for a singular identity, as all twins do. But the only way she knew to acquire that sense of a separate self was to lash out at her sister.

In our sessions, Holly blamed Samantha for belittling her, criticizing her, and ultimately abandoning her. And she blamed her would-be friends and her coworkers for the same reasons. My objective was to help Holly understand that her inability to take responsibility for her actions, her behavior, and her hurt feelings was rooted in her upbringing. Having compared their daughters and perceived them as opposites, typecasting one as "good" and the other "not as good," Holly and Samantha's parents had laid the groundwork for Holly's struggles. But I advised Holly that she could empower herself to change that scenario. During her therapy, I tried to help her become aware of situations that triggered her feelings of being less than her sister and find ways to manage and self-regulate these unpleasant states.

From Bad Twin to Singular Self

Holly and Samantha's parents believed that once Holly was in college, no longer being compared to her sister, she would thrive. Why didn't she? Because being a bad twin all those years had interfered with Holly's ability to form an authentic singular self that she could take with her out into the world. What she took with her instead was a sense of being victimized and maligned, an ongoing feeling that no one understands her, no one likes her, and she can't do anything about it. Her parents understandably hoped that things would turn around for Holly once she separated from her twin, but this hope was very unrealistic given Holly's history of inhabiting the bad-twin role.

In her book, *Exploring Twins*, British sociologist Elizabeth A. Stewart points out how popular culture sensationalizes and perpetuates twin stereotypes, including the good/bad twin dynamic:

> Films made for television . . . often focus on a perceived good/evil split between twin siblings. The plots often follow the script whereby the evil brother/sister tries to stamp out his good brother/sister. The former often fails as good triumphs over evil. Many of these television plots or themes are rather simplistic but help to reinforce stereotypes about twins.[2]

Holly wasn't trying to "stamp out" Samantha, but her inability to stamp out the comparisons to her "good twin" sister led to rage and resentment, confrontational behavior, depression, and a sense of helplessness. Her essential struggle with Samantha was not unlike that of good/bad twins portrayed in classic mythology. Mythological narratives from various cultures highlight the dyadic tension and opposition between twins. As Vivienne Lewin postulates, the story of Romulus and Remus metaphorically reflects the lengths to which a twin dares to go in the quest for an individual self:

> Romulus and Remus planned to build a city on the banks of the Tiber. Romulus plowed a furrow to establish the city boundary, and Remus impetuously jumped over it. Romulus killed Remus for his transgression. This deed represents the power struggle so common between twins and perhaps also illustrates the degree of tension and the threat to the sense of the individual self that some twins experience if personal boundaries are not observed.[3]

Holly's antagonistic behavior toward her sister and others was an unacknowledged attempt to carve out an individual identity in opposition to Samantha's good-girl persona. But acting out as the bad twin is not the same as developing an authentic self; Holly was still organizing herself in relation to the twinship. Our therapy sessions were concerned with helping Holly envision a path whereby she could discover her unique self.

After a number of sessions during which I listened attentively while Holly gave one excuse after another for why she was unable to patch things up with a friend, communicate effectively with coworkers, or understand a family situation from another's perspective, I posed this question to her: "Have you ever thought that there might be something that you are doing or not doing, whether you realize it or not, that keeps you in this situation where you're unable to feel better and unable to get along with people? What is it, do you think, that you might be contributing to this ongoing situation?"

Holly got mad at me for suggesting that she look at her own behavior. Her anger toward me exemplified negative transference, wherein the therapist becomes a twin to the client. So I became an adversarial twin to Holly, and she became enraged at me. She responded, "That's not true!

I'm not doing anything wrong. It's that other people treat me unfairly, and I'm the one being wronged—even by you! You just don't get it. Nobody does!"

In the context of our sessions, because she trusted me and our connection, Holly could safely scream and be angry. She could lash out at me—as the good twin to whom she had been in opposition for so long—and at the perceived onslaught by all those she encountered who had done her wrong. So she kept coming to therapy, she kept being angry, and she kept telling me I was wrong—that the troubles she encountered were not about her behavior. Other people were to blame.

After several sessions, getting angry at me gave Holly the capacity to dig deeper, to try to understand why she continued to blame others, to feel sad, and to feel bad about herself. My becoming the surrogate good twin whom she could attack and denounce gave her an opportunity to finally acquire some insight into her own self. Until that point, Holly's pronouncements had always been defensive: "It's them, not me!" Being able to reproach me as the good twin within the safe confines of our therapeutic relationship, she came to recognize that being set up as the bad twin had led to her self-loathing and sadness. Being saddled with the bad-twin role had interfered with her ability to feel acceptable and lovable, to feel that people would like her, and to feel that she could have some of the things that came to Samantha so effortlessly.

Armed with this new awareness, Holly could begin to focus on relinquishing the familiar yet detrimental role as the bad twin and to commence the challenging process of developing a differentiated self.

From Good Twin to Bad Twin

Although in the above case, Holly was perceived as the bad twin and maintained that role into adulthood, sometimes the roles twins play in childhood can be reversed, leaving both adult twins confused.

Glen called me because he was agonizing over a situation with his twin brother, Frank. Frank, who is gay, and his lover had developed a close friendship with Glen's nineteen-year-old son, Dylan, who is also gay. Glen's concern was not that his brother and his son are gay; he was tormented by the belief that Frank was trying to steal his son from him.

Glen had always been the good twin. His parents blatantly favored him because he was the one who did well in school, and he was well liked by his many friends. Frank, on the other hand, was sullen and depressed, frequently acted out, and was essentially ignored by his parents. Glen mentioned that he felt slightly guilty for receiving all the attention and all the love from both his parents and his friends at school, but there was really nothing he could do about it.

After high school, Glen and Frank went to separate colleges, and in his first year of college, Frank came out as gay. The news was no big deal for either Glen or his parents. Frank had a series of boyfriends and was currently in a long-term relationship. Neither Frank nor his lover had children.

Over the years, the brothers had had an on-again, off-again relationship. Although they live in the same city, they would go for weeks without seeing each other and then would get together for lunch or a hike and enjoy their time together. Once in a while, an argument would crop up and "things would get kind of ugly," as Glen put it, but the two were fairly good friends.

The reason Glen phoned me in distress was that Dylan had recently started to hang out with Frank and his lover, and this was driving Glen crazy. He knew his response was irrational, but he couldn't feel comfortable with the growing closeness between his son and his brother. Glen would pick a fight with Frank when he heard that Frank invited Dylan and Dylan's boyfriend to join Frank and his lover for dinner or to go away for the weekend. This was happening with greater frequency; and what made things worse was that Glen was making his son feel guilty for wanting to be with Frank. Glen said, "I don't feel proud of the fact that I'm guilt-tripping my son. I honestly want him to do what he wants to do, but why does it feel like Frank is taking Dylan away from me?"

As in a triadic lover situation, Glen had become overly vigilant and suspicious, wondering "Is Dylan with Frank this weekend? What are they doing? Why am I being left out? Why doesn't my son love me anymore? Why does he love my brother more than me? Why am I being abandoned?"

How did the good-twin/bad-twin scenario figure into Glen's difficulty accepting his son's friendship with his twin brother? Having grown up as the successful good twin, Glen had a very limited experience with jealousy and insecurity. When it came to the twinship, he had never felt that he was anything less than number one, so he had never developed the ability to deal with feelings of being second rate, not the most important, or not the most lovable. Because of his son's attachment to Frank, Glen was now experiencing what it felt like to be the less-than twin, and his "guilt-tripping" behavior toward his son, as well as intense envy toward his brother, made him feel that the tables had turned and that he, not Frank, was the bad twin. Glen's jealousy and insecurity ran counter to his lifelong self-concept. He could no longer be the good twin if Dylan loved his uncle more than he loved his father.

Having been perceived as the good twin, Glen missed out developmentally on managing envy, resentment, and disappointment. Confronted with the sense that his twin brother was stealing the most important thing from him, Glen wasn't psychologically prepared to manage his feelings. He knew intellectually that he was overreacting, but that didn't help him handle what he was going through emotionally.

In our sessions, Glen and I talked about the good/bad twin split and how his insecurity about his son's growing closeness to Frank was an opportunity for Glen to reflect on the nature of the twinship. Since the competition for Dylan's love had made Glen feel vulnerable, I helped him acknowledge what Frank, as the less favored twin, might have experienced as he was growing up. During our discussions, Glen was able to feel more compassion for what Frank must have gone through as the less-than twin: "I know I wasn't very helpful to him then. I wasn't exactly compassionate or nurturing. I guess I was just in my own little bubble and wasn't really worrying about Frank feeling less loved or left out."

Glen felt that in some way, Frank's relationship with Dylan was payback: "I'm having a really, really hard time with Dylan and Frank becoming so close. And I know it's irrational, but I feel like I'm being punished for having had it easier when we were younger."

An important part of resolving the triadic conflict was making sure that Glen explained to Dylan what was going on. It was clear that Dylan was well aware of the animosity, jealousy, and competition between his father and his uncle, and because his dad had always been understanding and accepting, he had openly wondered. "What's wrong with you, Dad? You've never acted like this before!"

I encouraged Glen to sit down with Dylan and talk to him about his feelings and the reasons that he was so conflicted. So Glen revealed to his son how terribly ashamed he was of his jealous feelings. Being able to candidly express his feelings to Dylan about a situation that had caused him such anguish was indeed healing.

In therapy, Glen had repeatedly talked about how ashamed he was to admit that he was envious of his brother's friendship with his son. Understanding that his jealousy had its roots in the particular characteristics of the twinship helped Glen accept his feelings and become more comfortable with a situation that had been so distressing. Openly reflecting on the good/bad roles he and Frank had embodied throughout their lives enabled Glen to work toward accepting his son's friendship with Frank without agonizing fear or anger.

A Bad Twin's Righteous Anger

In the two previous stories, the twins' parents expressed some degree of favoritism early in their children's lives, so the twins took on their roles as good twin and bad twin in childhood. But what happens when the twins' roles diverge after they become teenagers?

Growing up in a traditional family, identical twins Justine and Denise were expected to be "good girls." The better they behaved, the better their grades, and the more compliant they were with the goals their parents set for them, the more assured they became of receiving their parents' approval. Their designated role in the family was to be good daughters and to fulfill their parents' expectations.

As children, the girls followed the rules precisely and never disappointed their parents. In high school, however, Justine finally dared to deviate from the prescribed parental plan. While most parents would be thrilled if their teen decided to "rebel" in the way Justine did, her parents were irate. It seems that Justine's rebellious decision to run for student body treasurer was an affront to her parents' ideas regarding what was and what was not an appropriate use of her time. When she won the election and had to spend several hours a week after school to fulfill her duties as treasurer, her parents repeatedly reprimanded her for disrupting their driving schedule. Nonetheless, Justine maintained her position in spite of her parents' annoyance and disapproval. Being on the student council was something she really enjoyed, and she adamantly refused to give it up.

Denise stayed out of the fray—neither voicing support for her sister nor overtly backing her parents. As I learned when they later sought therapy to help them resolve their relationship problems, the girls' twinship had always been fairly peaceful but not close. During the student council controversy, Denise realized that Justine was deviating from the "good girl" mold, but she did not change her own behavior. Denise stayed the course, following the familiar parental guidelines without complaint.

Justine's next act of rebellion came when she was a freshman in college and she proclaimed that she was majoring in political science. It seems her stint in high school government, as well as college activities she had become involved in, had sparked an interest in politics. Again, her parents were livid. Their plan for the girls was to choose majors that would lead to health careers, preferably via medical school.

Despite her parents' condemnation and negativity, Justine stuck to her guns and focused on political science classes. She did extremely well and was glad that she had chosen a path that represented what she really wanted to do. But there was a price to pay. Angry that Justine had diverged from the educational route they had intended for her, her parents told her that if she wanted to continue as a political science major, they would not pay her tuition for the following year. She would have to finance her education herself. Unable to come up with the funding to continue studying at the college she had been attending, Justine was forced to transfer to a community college. Over a period of several months, she sank into a depression that continued to worsen.

Her depression led to a threatened suicide, and then Justine made a token suicidal attempt. At that point the family went into family therapy, with Justine being the identified patient. The therapy lasted for only a few sessions and was not beneficial. According to both Justine and Denise, none of the family members were able to be honest about their feelings, and the parents had no idea what was going on with Justine. They were seemingly annoyed at the disruption her emotional breakdown had caused.

Eventually, Justine got back on her feet, finished college, and got a job related to her course of study. When they came to see me, the sisters were living together but did not consider each other friends. In fact, they were primarily interested in figuring out how to remedy a relationship that had become acrimonious. Denise said, "Everybody expects us to be best friends because we're twins—but we're not. We're not even close."

They were increasingly getting on each other's nerves and unable to find a way to break the pattern.

In their initial sessions, not only did I learn what had led to Justine's breakdown, but it became clear that beginning in high school, Justine's failure to conform made her parents so angry that she became the bad twin in their eyes. By running for student council, majoring in political science, and going against her parents' wishes, Justine had disappointed and enraged them. From that point on, the parents identified Justine as a troublemaker and inferior to Denise. After Justine's emotional trials, weakness was added to the parents' list of their daughter's perceived faults.

Justine revealed the extent to which her parents' disapproval had escalated: "My parents don't even trust me . . . they talk about me with Denise behind my back and consider me somehow flawed."

Her accusation was indeed valid. Leaving Justine out of the conversation, the parents had taken Denise aside and told her the location of the key to their safety deposit box. The reason: they felt that Justine was not able to adequately take care of family business matters. When Justine found out, she was upset that her parents perceived her as less trustworthy and less stable than Denise.

In our sessions, I validated Justine's sense of righteous anger over her parents' disapproval of her for pursuing her own interests. I told her, "How unbelievably hurtful it must have felt that your parents chastised you for choosing your own path." I helped Justine to appreciate, however, that in becoming the bad twin, she had attempted to assert herself and define her feelings. Although she got punished for it, she had made a life-changing decision to develop a singular self. It turned out that being bad was a good choice.

On a number of occasions in their therapy, Justine criticized her sister for not standing up for her during her college crisis. But Denise protested, "Our parents were demanding one thing; you were demanding another. The whole scene was crazy-making!" Caught in a loyalty conflict, Denise had negative feelings about her parents and her sister, but at the time she felt too paralyzed to react or respond. She had not yet had the opportunity to articulate the complicated conflictual feelings that she experienced growing up as a twin. She had to work through a tangle of confusion and despair to be able to understand herself and her twinship with clarity and accountability.

Getting to Know Each Other

Interestingly, when the sisters first came to therapy, Justine wasn't particularly emotional about the presenting problem of constant bickering with and animosity toward Denise. However, whenever we talked about Justine's depression or her suicide attempt (which had occurred several years prior to their seeing me), Justine would cry because Denise had failed to stand up for her and because her parents had made it so hard for her to choose the college program she wanted. Each time she cried, we were able to work through Justine's feelings about how hard it had been for her, how much she suffered, how she felt so alone, and how no one had been there to support her. I told Justine, "You understood what you needed, but nobody listened, nobody cared. You felt alone and abandoned, and in addition, you were labeled the identified patient and the bad twin in comparison to Denise."

Justine had never had the chance to have a cathartic response to the incidents that led to her emotional breakdown, to talk about what she had gone through and how much she had suffered. During our sessions, as Denise watched Justine talk about these events, she would tear up. She definitely felt bad for Justine, and her empathy was obvious. At one point, as Justine accused her of not stepping in and helping her, Denise sadly and quietly replied, "I couldn't. I tried, but there was nothing I could do." I could tell that Denise's empathic response during that session—the tears and the simple words "I tried"—allowed Justine to finally believe that her sister cared about her more deeply than she had previously assumed.

It was important for Denise to finally understand how her sister's conflict with her parents had led to her depression and suicidal episode. Although Denise had witnessed Justine's altered behavior during that period, Justine had never shared her feelings about what was going on internally. In fact, Justine was the less emotional of the two sisters, someone who generally kept her feelings to herself. So Denise never had the opportunity to fully appreciate what her sister had gone through as she made the transition from "good girl" to "bad twin."

Our therapy sessions were extremely helpful in enabling Justine to share those feelings with her sister. Denise witnessed Justine having emotions, being upset, and being a feeling person, and that experience very much altered her perception of and feelings toward her twin sister. While the sisters never expected nor necessarily desired to become best friends, I believe that their emotional honesty and depth of feeling during the therapy led to an authentic breakthrough in their relationship. The process wasn't easy for either of them, as that level of communication had never been a hallmark of their twinship.

Contrary to what many assume, even when twins spend more time with each other than with anyone else—as had been the case with Denise and Justine—they are not necessarily close emotionally. In fact, very often they have learned throughout their lives to be distant when together. Denise and Justine admitted that they didn't really know each other, that they didn't discuss or reveal their feelings, and that in many ways they felt like strangers. But they wanted to change that dynamic, which is why they entered therapy.

The reason the sisters had never been close is that they had no idea who they were as individuals. They were programmed to be twins, to be good girls, to get along with each other, and to live out the expectations and fantasies of their family, which they both did when they were younger.

They knew each other only as a twin sister, but that didn't have an internal meaning because they didn't have access to very much of their internal life. And unless you know yourself, you can't really know someone else—even your twin.

Not until Justine broke away from the itinerary laid out by her parents did she begin to know herself. Even her emotional turmoil led to self-examination and reflection. For Denise, being away from her parents and Justine during college allowed her to begin to discover who she was, but it was a tumultuous time. Because she is not as outgoing or sociable as Justine, for the first few years away at school she had a lot of social anxiety and difficulty making friends. However, even with these personal struggles, she came to know more about herself as an individual.

Having begun the process of individuation before they came to therapy, and having the desire to deepen their relationship through their sessions with me, the sisters were finally able to meet each other as separate individuals and to begin to find out who the other really was.

Beyond Black-and-White Thinking

Labeling same-age siblings according to how they appear to differ from each other is, unfortunately, a common practice among parents and friends of twins. In an effort to differentiate the two, they use black-and-white thinking to define each as the precise opposite of the other. The good/bad dynamic is an offshoot of this oppositional method of categorizing twins, with one twin personifying particularly good traits the other not-so-good or bad qualities. For example, one twin may be perceived as easygoing and the other as demanding; one as outgoing, the other as withdrawn; one as self-sufficient, the other as needy.

Although singletons are also frequently compared to their siblings, because they are not part of a dyad, their sense of self is more individuated from early on; therefore, comparative labels don't tend to define their identity. For same-age siblings, however, freeing themselves from a self-image that is engendered by ongoing comparisons to their twin can become an enormous challenge.

Parental labeling is not always responsible for initiating black-and-white distinctions between twins. Sometimes, in an attempt to be perceived as separate from a same-age sibling, a twin will choose an identity that is in stark contrast to that of his or her twin. Becoming a rebel to be seen as "not my high-achieving twin," for example, can be a way to ensure a unique identity.

In Holly's case, the bad/good characterizations of her and her sister became almost indelible, to the extent that Holly found it nearly impossible to relinquish her role as a maligned victim. Witnessing the ease with which her sister, Samantha, made friends and navigated social situations, Holly felt herself to be at the extreme opposite end of the social spectrum. Harshly comparing herself to her well-liked and admired sister, Holly perceived herself as an unappreciated, perennial scapegoat. Her ongoing behavior, aided by her parents' overprotection, reinforced the "less than my twin" identity that Holly had unwittingly developed. After our sessions enabled her to break through her anger and consider the part she played in maintaining her bad-twin persona, Holly could realistically look forward to developing a self that was not reliant on being Samantha's opposite.

As the twin who had always been seen as the good sibling, Glen faced a different challenge: dealing with unfamiliar feelings of jealousy and insecurity brought on by his twin's close relationship with Glen's son. Since Glen had always felt secure in his role as number one in the twinship, he was confounded by the sense of being demoted to second place and by his own unfair behavior toward his son and his brother. In therapy, he had the opportunity to reflect on what his twin, Frank, must have gone through earlier in life as the less-than twin and to develop more compassion toward him. Glen was also able to begin working on the coping skills necessary for managing envy, resentment, and disappointment. Having previously held the position of the good twin, he had missed out developmentally on acquiring those skills.

For Justine, being designated the bad twin by her parents didn't happen until relatively late in her childhood. Having previously shared the good-girl role with her twin sister, Justine made a decision in high school to rebel against her parents and chart a scholastic path that reflected her own interests. Consciously deciding to become the bad twin had life-threatening consequences for Justine; her parents' harsh response to her rebelliousness resulted in her depression and suicidal thoughts. But defying her parents' mandate to follow the good-twin path also had a positive effect. It strengthened Justine's sense of a singular self and later led Justine and her sister, Denise, to seek therapy to confront and resolve difficulties in their relationship. Although they had never been close, during therapy, Justine was finally able to openly express her feelings surrounding a traumatic period in her life, Denise was able to empathize with her twin, and a newfound closeness began to develop between the sisters.

In each of these cases, the therapeutic process involved coming to a deep understanding of what it means to cultivate a personal identity apart from one's twin. Renouncing the inclination to define oneself in relation to and in opposition to one's twin was fundamental, as was getting beyond good twin/bad twin black-and-white thinking.

CHAPTER 4

Caretaker/Cared-For

Naomi was organized by an ongoing mantra: "I will always take care of Nina. I will do this by making sure she comes in first, by letting her be the one who is more popular, by letting her get and be and do exactly what she wants. I will not get in the way. I will not do anything that could create conflict with Nina. I know that by doing all of this I can assure myself that Nina will always be there for me, will always have my back, and will always be my best friend."

Because of unrealistic yet prevailing parental and societal expectations, twins feel enormous pressure to not only get along but also maintain a resilient best-friend relationship. At the same time, the natural tendency to engage in twin rivalry can seriously threaten a positive connection between the siblings. So how does a twin find a way to stay happily connected to a same-age sibling when confronted with constant comparative judgments about his or her relative position in the twinship? Taking on the role of caretaker can provide a solution.

In Naomi's case, even though Nina had a more domineering personality, Naomi became the caretaker by standing aside and allowing Nina to shine. She took care of Nina by ensuring her sister's success and sacrificing her own. Naomi considered it her role to be the facilitator of whatever it took to make Nina happy.

Born into a family in which the parents fought constantly, Naomi grew to fear conflict of any sort—especially conflict with Nina, on whom her life depended. She figured out that the best way not to have fights or conflict was to let Nina win everything. In discussing their early relationship, Naomi said, "I consciously took a backseat. I always was in second place. I wanted to do that, I deliberately did that, because I was happy if Nina was happy. And I was happy that there were no fights."

As Naomi revealed to me during her therapy sessions, her caretaking role with Nina served two functions: it prevented conflict between them and it helped maintain their sacred connection. All Naomi had to do was to make sure that Nina was number one. For her part, Nina had no trouble being in the limelight. Having been shown favoritism by her parents for her winning accomplishments and strong personality, she received more attention and felt naturally entitled to it. As a child and adolescent, Naomi didn't resent giving over any attention to Nina and making sure that Nina got what she wanted. She liked being the caregiving person. And she believed it would continue to result in a big payoff: being Nina's best friend forever.

That bubble burst when, in their senior year of college, Nina got a boyfriend.

After All I've Sacrificed for You

That's when Naomi came to see me. The presenting problem was that Naomi was so angry and so depressed over Nina's new relationship with her boyfriend, Colin, that Naomi was having what she described as a "meltdown." Nina's decision to pair up with Colin felt to Naomi "like an unexpected death." Everything she had done and sacrificed for Nina, everything she had felt and believed about their unbreakable connection, seemed completely shattered. Nina's connection to Colin meant that Nina had no connection with Naomi anymore. For Naomi, the situation was completely black and white: Colin had taken her place in Nina's life. Naomi had been abandoned. Naomi was unlovable.

When I asked what the sisters' relationship had been like prior to Nina's getting a boyfriend, Naomi described it as having been "hearts and flowers and rainbows." She said that she had never before had any ambivalent feelings toward her sister. It was all wonderful, all good. Although they attended separate colleges, they had been in touch daily. "I had a few casual friendships at college, but I never was really concerned about having friends because I had Nina," she said. Now the connection that meant the most to her—that meant everything to her—had been destroyed, according to Naomi, and she was having a hard time functioning. During our first session, she was inconsolable.

At our next session, Naomi cried uncontrollably. She felt alone and bereft and said that she couldn't even be at the same table with Nina when they had dinner at their parents' house. It was too upsetting. In fact, she said, "I don't even recognize her anymore. She's not my sister. How can I rely on her from now on?"

I asked Naomi if it might be a good idea for Nina to come to the next session. I said, "You've been so overwhelmed and unable to explain to Nina what you're going through. If she comes to a few therapy sessions, I can be a voice, a witness. I can help put into words what you're so upset about because I know that it's very hard for you to articulate it given that you have so many feelings about Nina and this new situation with her boyfriend."

In fact, those feelings had been so overwhelming for Naomi and she cried so much that she had filled a wastebasket with tissues during each of those first few sessions. Often she couldn't even talk; all she did was cry. She agreed to have Nina come to the next few sessions.

At their joint session, Naomi was initially unable to stop crying, so I began by telling Nina, "I know that it probably doesn't make sense to you that Naomi is so upset about your having a boyfriend. I know that it must be hard for you to understand because you're not organized in the way that Naomi is. But her response and her feelings are not about an objective reality; they are about a subjective perspective. What's making Naomi upset is her own feelings about how things have changed between the two of you."

Then Naomi tried to express to Nina how outraged she was that Nina couldn't empathize with her side of the boyfriend situation: "How can you not see things from my side? You're leaving me, you've got a boyfriend now, and you can't even tell me that you understand how I feel! I've always been there for you—why can't you be there for me now? Why don't you understand what I'm going through?"

Nina was clearly taken aback by Naomi's outburst: "What the hell are you talking about? I never asked you to 'be there for me'! I don't even know what you're talking about. I'm sorry that you're so upset, but I don't know why you're holding me responsible for your depression. Do you want me to break up with my boyfriend?"

Basically, Nina was saying "Get over it." Although it was painful for Naomi, it was important for her to hear what Nina had to say because it was a reality check. Prior to the joint session, Naomi was lost in her own thoughts and feelings about the perceived "breakup" of her relationship with Nina, what her role as caretaker had always meant, and what she thought the payoff was going to be. Hearing her sister express her own subjective perspective about Naomi's response to the boyfriend situation allowed Naomi to finally understand that Nina not only had a very limited capacity to be empathic but also did not feel the same way about the alleged emotional obligations of their twinship. It was as if they were thinking and speaking in two different languages.

The session was significant because Naomi began to see how her sister really thinks and feels and responds in a way that she had probably never been able to see before because her previous understanding of Nina was clouded by her role as caretaker. Rather than simply wondering "How can Nina be so unsympathetic and unfeeling?" Naomi witnessed her sister acting that way, which became a defining moment. Also, I was there to observe Nina's response to what Naomi was going through. So even though that session was painful for Naomi, it was validating.

Still, the fact that her sister didn't understand her perspective was a blow to Naomi. Not only did she feel abandoned and bereft because of Nina's relationship with Colin, but she was unable to work through her feelings without any dyadic empathic understanding from Nina—and therefore unable to attain a degree of closure. Although initially, both sisters had thought it would be beneficial for Nina to come to several sessions, Naomi didn't want Nina to come to therapy anymore because recognizing Nina's lack of sympathy was so distressing.

In our next session, I validated Naomi's feelings of disappointment and outrage: how upsetting it must be that her sister did not get her, that Nina seemed not to care about or understand what Naomi was going through, that Nina could not be empathic. I explained to Naomi that Nina is not organized like Naomi, which is why she is unable to be concerned about Naomi's feelings. Nina doesn't understand why Naomi is so upset because Nina is focused on herself and is not psychologically oriented.

We discussed the impact that Naomi's caretaking likely had on the sisters' relationship and on Nina's perspective and behavior. Given that Naomi had always taken care of Nina by ensuring that she was number one, Nina believes that she is entitled to whatever she wants—in this case, a boyfriend—without worrying about how that affects anyone else.

Our discussion helped explain why Nina is self-involved and has a limited capacity to take in Naomi's perspective and feelings. However, it was also important for us to further explore how Naomi had become a caretaking twin in the first place.

Reverse Parenting and Pathological Accommodation

During Naomi's therapy, I learned that she was a caretaker not only to her sister but to her mother as well. Sensitive to her mother's needs and moods, Naomi has always been there whenever she feels her mother is vulnerable or upset. If a conflict of any sort arises, or if Naomi sees that her mother is angry or worried, she jumps in, thinking that her job is to soothe and take care of her mother. I explained to Naomi that this type of behavior is often referred to as *reverse parenting*. When a child isn't getting what he or she needs, to avoid feeling abandoned or angry, the child may handle the situation by taking care of the parent in the hopes of fostering a meaningful connection. So how did this dynamic between Naomi and her mother likely develop?

Naomi had said that when she and Nina were born, Nina came home from the hospital with her mother, but Naomi stayed in the newborn intensive care unit; Nina weighed five pounds and Naomi weighed only three. I shared with Naomi that what likely occurred, as it very often does in similar situations, is that their mother became attached to Nina but lacked an adequate attachment to Naomi. That is because when the mother of twins brings home only one baby, attaches to that twin, and then days later brings the second one home, the second twin may be unconsciously perceived as an outsider or intruder. The mother may have difficulty emotionally readjusting herself to the appearance of the second baby. I brought this up with Naomi, sharing with her that because her mother had already attached to newborn Nina, Naomi's appearance was quite possibly met with anxiety and a lack of sufficient nurturing and attention.

So as a small child, Naomi probably reacted not only by attaching to her sister but by acting as a caretaker to her mother as well. Needing yet lacking an adequate attachment to her mother, she became her mother's caretaker as a way to feel connected to her. It became a role that Naomi still inhabits, and the reverse parenting continues.

When a child has to take on the needs and feelings of a parent and is thus unable to work through his or her own feelings, it results in trauma and a personality that is disorganized. I believe that's what happened in Naomi's case. Taking care of her sister was also a way to take care of her mom because Naomi was taking over the burden of looking after Nina. But when you always have to be there for somebody else—overempathizing and overaccommodating—you are left with no self. You're traumatized because you have no sense of yourself as a secure person with needs and feelings of your own.

Once the focus of her therapy was no longer about blaming Nina, Naomi began to ask, "What's wrong with me? How did I get myself into this mess? How could I have allowed myself to be so out of touch with my sister and the reality of my life?" One way to explain the reality of her life—the "mess" to which she referred—is to consider what Dr. Bernard Brandchaft identified as *pathological accommodation*. Throughout her life, Naomi had accommodated her feelings, her behavior, her intentions, and her goals in such a way as to ensure her sister's success and happiness. If Nina was happy, Naomi was happy—even if it meant that Naomi sacrificed her sense of self. Dr. Brandchaft was not referring to twins when he described such behavior; however, his characterization of the systems of pathological accommodation helps explain what often takes place in a caretaker/cared-for twinship.

Dr. Shelley R. Doctors defines Brandchaft's thinking in her article entitled "Brandchaft's Pathological Accommodation—What It Is and What It Isn't":

> Pathological structures of accommodation, the organizing principles that develop in contexts in which one unconsciously sacrifices one's own perceptual-emotional reality and adopts that which is required by an "other" to maintain a needed tie, come into being amidst great anxiety.... Interferences with or changes to organizing principles developed to preserve an attachment bond threaten the coherence

and continuity of the self-organization created in the context of that relational bond.[1]

Naomi did indeed adopt Nina's reality to maintain the "needed tie" that bound the two together. That reality involved Naomi's providing the necessary caregiving behavior that would ensure Nina's number-one status. Although Naomi acknowledged having made sacrifices to take care of her twin in this way, she said that she did so gladly. Avoiding the type of conflict she witnessed between her parents by preventing disagreements with Nina also figured into Naomi's motivation. Although deferring to Nina when the two were very young was likely unconscious, as they grew older, Naomi's caretaking bargain was consciously and happily entered into, as she reaped the benefits of being Nina's closest confidante and best friend.

The pathology inherent in this accommodating dynamic became apparent when Naomi could barely function upon hearing that Nina was no longer holding up her end of the bargain. Naomi wanted to continue to be her sister's caretaker, but a boyfriend was now taking her place in Nina's primary relationship. Having been organized to accommodate her life to her sister's, Naomi essentially fell apart when that lifelong organizational structure was rendered obsolete.

Shelley R. Doctors elaborates:

> "Accommodation" refers to the child's response to a relational trauma, trauma suffered when his or her emotional expressions and/or actions regularly evoke profoundly malattuned parental responses. We call this relational trauma because repeated, severe emotional disjunctions threaten the child's attachment bond to his caretaker, the relationship most critical to development.[2]

Emotionally Disconnecting

Naomi went through a period when she could not even talk to Nina. Nina would call or text and Naomi would not respond. She told me she felt "tormented," going back and forth between wanting to call Nina, missing her tremendously, wanting to reconnect and recapture "the way it was before Colin," and fighting that urge. She said she resisted the compulsion to text or call Nina because her feelings of abandonment were so intense, but she felt terribly lonely without any contact.

In therapy, we talked about how Naomi could learn to communicate with Nina by emotionally disconnecting from her somewhat. She could have shorter, easier, more superficial kinds of interaction so as not to fall back into her habitual pattern of completely giving herself over to Nina by listening to and supporting her. In other words, she could invest less in Nina and more in her own self-preservation. She could work at giving less of herself while also expecting less of Nina in the way of emotional support, something Nina had rarely provided.

We had a concrete deadline for accomplishing this goal: Nina's college graduation. Naomi wanted to be able to go to the graduation without falling apart. Facing this challenge would be hard for Naomi, given that the graduation would be the first time she would meet Colin and be confronted with seeing him and Nina together.

Naomi texted me during the graduation weekend to say that she had mostly succeeded. Although she had to leave the table briefly during the celebratory dinner to cry in the bathroom, overall she held up fairly well.

Because she has been in therapy, Naomi knows the extent to which she should stay engaged with Nina in conversations where everything is about Nina and her problems—asking Naomi for advice and using her as a sounding board. Depending on whether Naomi is in the mood to fill the role of supportive listener, she can decide to take on that function with Nina or not. Naomi has made progress in that she is fully conscious of the fact that she has always been Nina's caretaker but she now has a choice: she can decide when she wants to take care of Nina in that way. She is able to choose whether she wants to answer the phone or text Nina back. Also, she has learned to have very low expectations of her sister. Naomi is now more conscious of Nina's self-involvement and more realistic regarding the level of emotional support that Nina is capable of providing.

If Nina starts a conversation with "I've got to tell you what happened to me today!" Naomi will say, "Oh, do you want to hear about my day?" Naomi laughed when she told me this, and she's proud of the fact that she doesn't get triggered by Nina's self-centeredness anymore. She knows that's just who Nina is. And she makes sure to get off the phone if Nina starts dominating the conversation with her own concerns.

Naomi has made great strides in relinquishing her caretaking behavior with Nina, but certain aspects of that deep-rooted role remain. She recently told me that she was afraid of what would happen if Nina and Colin broke up: "I'm really afraid for Nina. I don't want them to break up because then Nina will be so unhappy." I said, "So?" And she responded, "Well . . . that would be terrible." I told her, "Boyfriends and girlfriends break up. It's not the end of the world. It happens."

Often I need to provide a reality check for Naomi. She has to realize that most people experience expectable as well as unpredictable ups and downs throughout their lives, instead of believing that she can and should be in control of everyone else's well-being. Naomi's sense of self will evolve as she recognizes the importance of focusing on her individual self.

Caretaking Friends

Throughout our initial sessions, Naomi expressed her essential feeling about her connection to Nina: "Nina is the most important person in my life, and I will never need another relationship." Although no one would ever take the place of her beloved sister, Naomi finally acknowledged the need for friends.

However, she tended to treat her friends as she had treated Nina; the caretaker role remains an enduring part of Naomi's identity. Naomi fears that if she doesn't defer to her friends' wishes, they will get mad at her or not like her, neither of which is easy for her to tolerate. She doesn't want anyone to be mad at her, and she can't stand conflict, which is why Naomi can't do what she would like to do. Instead, she feels that she must do what her friends expect her to do.

During one session, Naomi presented a conflict that is not uncommon for a twenty-four-year-old. Her friend Lucy had invited her to a party that started late. Naomi likes Lucy and wanted to go to the party with her, but she had to be up very early the next morning for an important work assignment. She felt that she couldn't turn down Lucy because she dreaded the thought of Lucy being mad at her. And Lucy told her that she wouldn't go to the party unless Naomi went with her.

I asked Naomi, "Wouldn't you be taking care of yourself if you actually did what you wanted to do rather than doing what Lucy wants you to do?" But whenever I brought up taking care of herself, being "selfish" in a positive way, or feeling entitled, Naomi understood the concept but couldn't get beyond merely understanding to actually transforming the concept into behavior. She defaulted to a self-denying, self-loathing self: "Why should I do something nice for myself? I don't deserve it." Sadly, Naomi didn't feel that she was a good enough person to give herself what she wanted or needed. In the context of the therapeutic setting, she would feel deserving for an instant, but then the unworthy, caretaking part of her took over.

I told her, "You seem to view your friendships in terms of caretaking—thinking that you have to be what your friend wants and give her what she needs, just as you did with Nina. Too often you end up feeling trapped and unfulfilled. Even though you don't mean to, you become the caretaker who doesn't take care of herself."

For Naomi, friendships resemble a twin attachment. She feels compelled to accommodate Lucy and other friends just as she always accommodated Nina's needs and desires. She is still conflicted about asking for what she wants and fearful of alienating her friends, just as she was fearful of alienating Nina. I told Naomi, "Taking on the caretaker role is how you organize yourself, and it is a repetition of how you gave up so much of yourself for Nina. If you don't try to move beyond this way of feeling and thinking, you'll continue to feel trapped and paralyzed. You'll need to take baby steps to try to make a change."

In a recent session, Naomi told me, "Joan, I hear everything you're saying, but I can't do it."

While Naomi finds it difficult to honor her own needs if it means disappointing a friend, she is making progress. She can now identify when she is repeating an old pattern of behavior or sinking into an unhealthy thought process. Although she may not be able to stop herself, she acknowledges that emotional shifts require time and patience. She is beginning to be more honest with a close friend and to tell her how she feels in the moment. She recently made a friend at work with whom she feels comfortable enough to want to become roommates, which is a good sign. And just the fact that she has tried and been able to make friends is a major step. In high school and college, Naomi never even tried. "I didn't need to make friends then," she said, "I had Nina."

Unreciprocated Selflessness

Although a twin who takes on the role of caretaker doesn't necessarily expect the cared-for twin to reciprocate in kind, when the imbalance between giving and receiving becomes extreme, a caretaker may feel angry and victimized. Such was the case with fraternal twins Paul and Perry.

Paul had been his brother's caretaker since grade school. He was the more dominant brother, and Perry was more accommodating. Paul made friends easily and encouraged Perry to join in once friendships were established. Both boys did well in school and seemed to excel in similar subjects, including art and math. Paul dated more than Perry in high school, but they both enjoyed hanging out with the same circle of friends. They attended the same college and the same professional school, and both became architects.

Their conflict originated when Paul persuaded Perry to move to a new city where Paul had secured a position with a prestigious architectural firm. Although Perry had yet to settle on which branch of architecture he would pursue and had nothing tying him down, he was unsure about the move. Paul's argument in favor of Perry's joining him was "I can't fathom living apart from you." He assured Perry that he would help him find a job in their new location. Perry went along with the move.

In their new city, Perry did not fare very well. Uncertain how to jump-start his career and feeling a lack of motivation and direction, he became very depressed. Paul felt bad that Perry was having a hard time and guilty about having pressured Perry to make the move. He spent all his free time devoting himself to Perry—researching job possibilities for him and trying to help him network and figure out what he should do next. Meanwhile, Paul was doing exceptionally well. At the end of his first year with the firm, he was to be honored, along with several others, at a special dinner. The day of the event, Perry told Paul that he could not make it as he was feeling extremely depressed. So Paul didn't go to the dinner; he stayed home to take care of Perry and make sure he was okay.

That was three years ago. Paul came to see me with two presenting issues: he had just broken up with his girlfriend because he found out that she cheated on him, and Perry had recently told him that he was getting married. The two issues dovetailed in that now Perry was unavailable when Paul needed him most. Paul said, "I get it that they're planning a wedding and spending every minute together, but doesn't he remember three years ago? He couldn't even rouse himself out of bed to go to the most important event in my career at that point! And I was there for him. That year when he couldn't find his way and was so depressed, I never went out, had no social life, and basically just devoted myself to him."

When we began to explore the brothers' history, it came to light that over the years, Paul had sacrificed his time and energy taking care of Perry, and he had often been disappointed at the lack of reciprocity. For example, when Paul was with his girlfriend, he would often invite Perry to join them when Perry was feeling down, making it a threesome. In fact, Paul admitted that the trouble with his girlfriend may have been related to her feeling that Paul was "too devoted" to his brother, something she had mentioned on a number of occasions.

When Paul confronted Perry about not being there for him during the breakup with his girlfriend, Perry (like Nina in the previous story) was oblivious to any wrongdoing on his part, saying "What are you talking about? What did I do? Why are you so angry?"

I told Paul: "While you may not have been able to acknowledge it, on some level you have known for many years what Perry is like—what he is able to give you and what he is incapable of giving you. So you have to decide if you are willing to accept the relationship on those terms. Are you able to alter your expectations and figure out a way to be with your brother where you don't feel like you're doing all the giving? It may mean that you will have to become less compassionate and less of a caretaker."

Giving up the unrealistic expectation that Perry would become as compassionate and caring as Paul had always been was not Paul's only challenge. We also considered the reality of Perry's current situation: he likely did not need Paul as much anymore. He had launched his professional life, he was getting married, and he had not been demonstrating the need to constantly check in with Paul as he had previously. I shared with Paul that giving up his function as caretaker to Perry would not be easy.

Caretakers aren't the only ones who can have unrealistic expectations. As the next case shows, the cared-for twin can develop feelings of entitlement that cripple his ability to become a well-rounded individual.

"How Dare You Deny Me the Help I Need!"

For twentysomething identical twins Devon and Seth, the presenting issue was an "insane fight" that they were unable to sort out.

After listening to their story in a video chat, I could see that Devon took for granted that his caretaker twin, Seth, would always be available for whatever Devon needed. The current conflict centered on a task that Devon wanted Seth to complete for him. He was sending out an important resume and expected Seth to help him write it. Seth refused. He didn't want to help Devon because, according to Seth, Devon had been "nasty and demanding." Seth told Devon, "You can't treat me this way. I'm not helping you with this or anything else. . . . I've had it!"

Devon was so incensed that he resorted to a radical measure to vent his anger: he called his parents, told them that Seth was sabotaging his career by not helping him, and insisted that they do something drastic to force Seth to comply. He told them, "I want you to cut off his internet and his phone." They did so.

Seth was understandably outraged, called home to tell his parents to reconnect his internet and phone, and also relayed his side of the story: Devon had treated him badly and, in any case, was entirely capable of writing the resume on his own.

The phone and internet were back on, but the issues between the brothers remained unresolved, namely, who was entitled to what and why?

What is most important about this story is the intensity of Devon's rage and dependency. Needing his brother to complete a task for him that he was capable of completing himself, being unable to accept Seth's negative response, and then harnessing his anger and desperation to persuade their parents to punish Seth, Devon behaved in ways that revealed how stuck he was in the role of entitled, overly dependent cared-for twin.

In our initial video chat, Devon vented his feelings, "How dare Seth deny me the help I needed! He knows he's much better at that kind of thing than I am. It was outrageous that he said no."

I offered my response: "It seems that Seth's saying no made you feel extremely violated. What you seem to be saying is, 'How dare Seth say no and neglect my needs.' It is as if you believe that Seth owes you his time whenever you need it."

Seth added, "And why would you go to such an extreme—even involving our mom and dad—for such a minor offense? It's unbelievable!"

In our next session, I asked the brothers to describe their childhood. Seth said, "Everybody at school—teachers and friends—treated us like a pair; no one knew who was who, so there was that stupid game of trying to tell us apart. We were never individuals."

When I asked Devon about how the brothers were treated at home, he said, "If we didn't get along, my mom would have a fit."

From their separate remarks, I discerned that their childhood consisted of Seth caretaking and sacrificing and Devon feeling dependent and entitled. I had the sense that Devon's notion of fairness throughout his youth and in the present resume-writing conflict boiled down to "You owe me."

Such outrage on the part of a cared-for twin who feels neglected by the caretaker is not unusual. In a sense, it can be seen as emotional battering. The entitled, cared-for sibling is telling the caretaker twin, "You don't get to say no to me, ever. No matter what I've done to you, no matter the circumstances, you owe me."

According to Seth, the boys' mother had always insisted that the two be best friends; not getting along was not okay. And throughout their childhood, Seth mostly took on his role stoically. I mentioned that often the fear of intense feelings, such as those Devon had expressed, keeps twins believing that they have to maintain harmony. Perhaps Seth and Devon had reached a point, however, where the effort to be falsely harmonious was crazy making.

I also shared my thoughts about the timing of their blowup. The intensity of Devon's reaction and the finality of Seth's proclaiming that he was done helping Devon most likely occurred because the brothers had only recently had the opportunity to be away from each other—during a spring break—and then had to reconnect as roommates. They had each had a taste of freedom, of getting in touch with their individuality, so coming together again probably intensified their conflict.

I had no further joint video chats with Devon and Seth, but I had individual sessions with each of them. Seth talked about having a lot of angry thoughts about being a twin and having to put up with his brother and how difficult it was for them to live together. He was planning to move out and live with a friend instead—and he was very much looking forward to that. Devon said he was fine with Seth moving out because they were "always fighting over stupid stuff. I think we're just sick of each other."

I didn't hear from either brother for several months, and then they both sent me short follow-up emails. Seth said how relieved he was to be living a separate life from Devon and how much he was learning about himself. Devon remarked that he missed Seth but added, "It's really great to meet people who don't even know I'm a twin."

Beyond Dominant/Passive

Labels can be deceiving. Although people often assume that the caretaker twin is the more dominant sibling, that's not necessarily the case. In twinships like Naomi and Nina's, for example, the caretaker is the quiet, submissive one who takes a backseat to her sibling and whose caretaking involves sacrificing her own needs and success to make sure that her twin can shine. Nina was the more dominant twin, and Naomi did everything she could to make that stick. In fact, she was dedicated to ensuring Nina's dominance. Naomi liked putting herself in second place because it made her feel that she was a good person. And she liked the fact that she allowed Nina to win because it gave her a function that she felt good about and that defined who she was.

In Paul and Perry's case, Paul was the more dominant, competent brother; Perry was more accommodating and less decisive. Paul was socially confident and Perry less so, yet Paul was the one who expressed that he couldn't fathom moving to a new city without Perry. Although Paul was the caretaker who took charge when Perry couldn't seem to get his life together, Paul was also the one who fell apart when his brother decided to get married.

Neither Seth nor Devon could be called passive or submissive. Both had strong personalities. Until his eventual breaking point when he declared he'd had enough, Seth had always made himself available to take care of Devon's every need. And Devon felt entitled to his brother's caretaking. In such cases, when the cared-for twin feels that he is owed his brother's ongoing help, the caretaking twin may be unaware that he is being taken advantage of and that he is enabling his brother's exploitative behavior.

So the caretaker/cared-for dynamic can take on various forms, some of which do not conform to the expectation that the caretaker is dominant or controlling and the cared-for twin is passive or submissive. What is most important in terms of treating twins is helping clients become aware of the roles they may have played in their twinship, how those roles developed, and how dismantling the caretaker/cared-for dynamic can benefit and liberate both parties.

Renouncing the Caretaker/Cared-For Dynamic

For adult twins who are organized according to the caretaker/cared-for dynamic, it can often be more difficult for the caretaker sibling to relinquish his role than for the cared-for twin. This is because the caretaker's identity is more deeply linked to a function he has performed for many years. Without it, the caretaker loses something that was not only a source of self-esteem—helping and guiding his sibling—but, more importantly, a defining piece of who he was as a sibling and as a person.

Naomi found it extremely challenging to give up her role as caretaker of her sister, Nina. When Naomi found out that Nina had a boyfriend, Naomi was rendered—in her mind—useless. Once Nina no longer needed her sister, Naomi's "job" was no longer required and her psychological function was eliminated. And without the function that she had performed for a lifetime, she no longer had a connection to her sister. So she lost Nina, she lost her function as caretaker to her sister, and most importantly, she lost what she felt was her role in the world, which was to be Nina's scaffold forever—holding up her sister and ensuring that she succeeded. When the boyfriend appeared, the scaffold collapsed and Naomi felt annihilated. That's why Naomi couldn't stop crying in our initial sessions. She felt a loss on so many levels that she couldn't stop asking herself, "Who am I? What am I supposed to do? How am I supposed to go through life?"

A similar dynamic was in play with Paul. Losing his function as caretaker meant that he faced a struggle to define who he was apart from his twin. His core identity was in question because the caretaking function had been a stand-in for a developed self. I explained to Paul that a healthy self has the capacity to handle difficult feelings and changes, and he would need to abandon his focus on his twin brother to develop that capacity. Having spent a lifetime overseeing Perry's well-being and depending on that function for a large part of his identity, Paul faced a challenge in relinquishing it.

In speaking to parents of twins at workshops and conferences, I am often asked how to help the cared-for twin become more independent from her caretaking sibling. Parents seem to express more concern for the child who has been on the receiving end of sibling nurturance than the one who has been providing it. I tell them that they probably need to focus more on their caretaking child because her emotional needs may have been severely neglected.

This comes as a surprise to parents who view the caretaker twin as more mature and less needy. But very often the needs of the caretaking twin have not been adequately met by the parents, which may be why she resorts to nurturing or overseeing her twin to feel some kind of close connection. The caretaking twin takes it upon herself to be there for her same-age sibling, but she often lacks emotional support and loving attention herself. Parents may be unaware of this deficiency in their caretaking child and of the fact that she is in danger of growing up to feel as if her only function is to take care of others. As the stories in this chapter reflect, a caretaker twin often struggles to develop a sense of self apart from her function of caring for someone else.

The caretaker/cared-for dynamic usually reaches a crisis point when one twin no longer feels comfortable fulfilling her role. The cared-for twin may tire of being nurtured or overseen by her sibling, even when such attention is lovingly offered. The caretaking twin may be "fired" from her job, sometimes as a consequence of the cared-for twin finding a romantic partner. Or the caretaking twin may finally grow weary of abdicating her own needs in favor of her sibling's.

While dismantling the caretaking/cared-for pattern can be a difficult and painful transition, it is absolutely necessary if both individuals are to become free to develop their unique selves.

CHAPTER 5

Crisis of Identity

When Alex came to see me, his presenting issue was the need to understand why he had put up with persistent emotional and physical abuse from his boyfriend. As described in chapter 1, Alex, as well as his twin brother, Brad, had never learned to process his feelings, having grown up protecting his mother from an abusive husband and being caught up in a reverse parenting dynamic. As for the brothers' relationship, Alex told me that he and Brad "didn't really discuss feelings." Nevertheless, their primary attachment was to each other. Now in their early thirties, they were quarreling a lot, which was another reason why Alex needed to talk to someone.

Alex was particularly distressed that Brad was shutting him out when he needed him most—during his difficult breakup with his boyfriend. Without Brad's "input and guidance," Alex said that he was "completely lost." I asked Alex to explain how he had come to depend on input from Brad and why his brother's guidance was so crucial.

He said, "I could never do anything wrong as a kid, even if I wanted to, because Brad was there and he would tell on me. I never had a life of being by myself, ever. So I couldn't do anything wrong because my conscience—Brad—was always right there, keeping me in line. I didn't really think about it then, but I couldn't do anything without Brad knowing what I was doing. Even if he didn't say anything, Brad always knew, and I knew that he knew."

It was as if Brad's role as Alex's "conscience" completed Alex, made him whole. Having this internalized judge inside him meant that Alex would never do anything that he knew his brother would be critical or disapproving of. And without the need for any conversation between them, Alex became adept at anticipating Brad's every potential judgment of him.

He recalled how his social behavior in college was wordlessly overseen by Brad: "Even if I had done my work, I knew that Brad would be critical if I wanted to go away for the weekend . He wouldn't have to say anything, he wouldn't have to do anything, but I'd know that he would be thinking, 'How can you possibly be going away for the weekend when you have a paper due on Monday?' So even though I knew it was okay for me to go because my paper was complete, just the fact that he was judging me, even if it was never said, meant that I would never have allowed myself to go."

Brad filled in pieces that Alex felt were missing in himself. Alex had always taken for granted that his brother was a part of him in an essential way, and thus he always had the mentality of a *we-self*.

Complementarity and the We-Self

Dr. Dale Ortmeyer refers to a "complementarity of mutually shared aspects of personality, a we-self" and to "the unhealthy aspects of this complementarity."[1] In her book *The Twin in the Transference*, Vivienne Lewin summarizes Ortmeyer's concept of the we-self and twin complementarity:

> Ortmeyer postulates that . . . twins develop a psychological unity, a 'we-self' system instead of an individual identity. There is insufficient distinction between one twin's personality and the other's. The two personalities blend in such a way that some traits are complementary, i.e. non-duplicative and non-identical. These traits endure and each twin will have particular traits more fully

developed and structured than the other twin. The twins do not distinguish between their own and their twin's personality but instead use each other's personality as an adjunct to their own. Each twin will therefore experience difficulties at an individual level . . . The absence of the other twin creates anxiety that may become acute, because of the loss of certain personality traits that are needed for the individual twin to function.[2]

Within Alex and Brad's we-self was a shared sense of what was okay and what was not. But once Alex moved in with his boyfriend, Brad was not as available to be his brother's conscience. Without Brad's unspoken guidance, Alex lost his sense of right and wrong, which in turn may have contributed to his failure to acknowledge how abusive his boyfriend was.

Although the brothers grew up with an abusive stepfather, which potentially laid the groundwork for one or both of them to become involved in an abusive relationship, for Alex, Brad's near absence from his life became the tipping point. Without the stabilizing effect of the we-self, Alex subjected himself to a reenactment of the alcoholic abuse that his mother had put up with and that Alex and Brad were supposed to protect her from.

Prior to Alex's romantic involvement, the brothers had not only spent time together every day but also phoned and texted each other throughout the day. They had an ongoing, structured plan for where and when they would meet up and what activities they would do together. When Alex initially became close with his boyfriend, the brothers maintained most of their mutually agreed-upon routine, and they even went out socially with their respective boyfriends. But then Brad began to pull away from Alex, and their relationship shifted dramatically.

After Alex moved in with his boyfriend, the brothers no longer engaged in their daily ritual of going to the gym and hanging out together on weekends. Since Alex is a very structured, almost compulsive person, the loss of that daily structure was perhaps even more important than the actual loss of his brother's company. The structure, routine, and predictability of their being together had been crucially important to Alex's sense of identity.

At the point that his split-up with his abusive boyfriend brought Alex to therapy, he had to reorganize his entire sense of himself because he didn't know who he was without his brother. He said that their present "almost nonexistent" relationship felt like "shock and awe"—to the extent that Brad appeared to be a different person. Alex kept stressing "This is not who Brad really is. It's not really him. I don't recognize this person."

Not only did Brad seem like an entirely different person to Alex, but disconnecting from the dyad—and from the we-self—was causing Alex to feel out of control and unsure about how his relationship with Brad was going to transition into something different. Severely depressed and "freaking out" because Brad was withdrawing from him and no longer interested in him the way that he used to be, Alex was having a crisis of identity.

Alex told me, "I don't know who I am. I don't know what I'm going to do. I've lived my whole life with him. Now what?" It seemed to Alex that he and Brad suddenly were not getting along, whereas they were getting along fine before. He told me they were having terrible fights, and I could tell that he did not have the capacity to work through his feelings with Brad.

I also learned that Brad had gone into therapy before Alex came to see me and that Alex felt that his brother's therapy had somehow put a wrench in their relationship: "He's just not the same ever since he's been going to therapy. He ignores me, doesn't want to be with me. I feel like he doesn't even like me anymore."

When they did get together, their interaction would often evolve into a fight. Alex would tell his brother, "I'll do anything to make you stay in a good mood. Tell me what I can do."

Alex tried to accommodate Brad's detachment to avoid conflict, but I had the sense that Brad wasn't really interested in being with his brother anymore. Alex was anxious and overwhelmed by this unforeseen turn of events. He wanted to figure out some way to reboot his previous in-sync relationship with Brad, but he was at a loss as to how to do that. Brad had changed, and Alex's attempts to keep things the same between them were sadly in vain.

I believe that being in therapy had helped Brad get out of the rut of his brotherly routine. He probably didn't like having to be accountable to Alex and no longer wanted the responsibility for being his twin brother's well-meaning conscience. Brad was in the process of moving on.

Confronting the Turmoil

Alex was motivated to go to therapy not only because he needed help understanding his abusive relationship with his boyfriend but also because he was clearly lost without Brad. The fact that Brad was seeing a therapist inspired Alex to see me. He felt that whatever was going on in Brad's therapy was creating a rift between the two of them, but he hoped that seeing a therapist himself might help him confront the emotional turmoil surrounding his abusive boyfriend, his unsympathetic brother, and his own sense of disequilibrium. Alex was suffering. He had lost his boyfriend, his twin, and his core identity. He felt abandoned, depressed, confused, and ashamed.

Alex had never told Brad about the abuse. In fact, he had never told anyone until he told me in therapy. He had so much shame and self-hatred regarding how he had allowed the abusive relationship to go on for so long. I think he felt an enormous sense of relief that he could finally talk about what happened with his boyfriend and how he could have allowed it to happen. When I suggested that there was a connection between the trauma that occurred in his own family (with his abusive stepfather) and the traumatic relationship with his boyfriend, Alex confessed that he had never put the two scenarios together because the abuse his mother suffered was never discussed. No one in his family ever talked about what all of them had witnessed and gone through. So Alex had never processed any of it.

As we talked about the abusive behavior of both his stepfather and his boyfriend, Alex began to recognize that what he lived with and how he coped growing up had led to his being dissociated from the abuse he suffered in his own relationship. He was very relieved to have someone help him recognize the reasons for the dissociation and the repetition of abuse and help him realize that he didn't have to repeat that abusive scenario.

We also had to confront the radical shift in Alex and Brad's twinship dynamic, so I wanted to know more about their childhood and what their relationship had been like prior to Alex's intense relationship with his boyfriend. I asked Alex to talk about the different roles he and Brad might have played growing up. Was Brad more social? Was Alex more organized? I was curious as to the complementarity of their strengths and weaknesses and how that may have led to a kind of shared identity. Given that Alex was so distraught over the loss of Brad's "input and guidance," it was likely that a we-self had been disrupted.

From what Alex revealed to me, it became clear that the brothers are structured in very different ways. Brad is much more comfortable being around people. Alex tends to be anxious around people. Brad doesn't need to have control over his surroundings; he doesn't mind a messy apartment or disruptive roommates. Alex is very particular about his personal environment and definitely needs his own space. Brad has no problem being who he is. Alex feels like he becomes someone else in certain situations.

Alex gave me a recent example of feeling like he becomes someone else. A friend of his told him how smart and thoughtful he is and that he wanted to spend more time with him. Alex panicked. When I asked him why, he said, "When I'm with someone and they're giving me a compliment or they say they want to be with me, I become somebody else. I lose all my ability to stay connected to my real feelings. I am no longer the person that I know, that I authentically feel. I become this person that the friend says he wants to be with."

Alex also mentioned that he feels terribly embarrassed when anyone gives him a compliment. So I wondered if something about being acknowledged in a positive way—whether it's being told by a friend that he wants to spend more time together or being given a simple compliment—makes Alex uncomfortable.

I said, "Maybe that discomfort is related to the twinship. Maybe that's what you always felt growing up whenever you were singled out. Anytime someone alluded to a difference between the two of you or gave you a compliment or gave you something more than your brother, maybe there was a disruption of the twinship, which caught you off guard."

Alex admitted that compliments make him feel strange: "When someone gives me a compliment, I don't know what to say and I don't feel like myself." He also shared that sometimes in middle and high school, his report cards "showed more As than Brad's," but he never wanted his mother to notice. (In fact, she was too involved with her own problems to pay much attention to her sons' grades.) I pointed out that by receiving As on his report card or a compliment from a friend, he was being acknowledged as an individual, distinguished from his brother. In other words, he was being singled out. But when someone is part of an enmeshed twin couple, being singled out can leave the person feeling anxious and uncertain. He doesn't know how to feel or what to think because he's not accustomed to being single—or singled out. He's anxious because he doesn't know who he is apart from the same-age sibling who completes his identity.

Alex remembered an incident in high school when he got the lead in a school play and Brad had a lesser role: "I don't remember whether or not I was good in the play. I think the school paper reviewed it pretty well, but I didn't really enjoy the whole experience. I kept thinking about

Brad and that it wasn't a good idea for me to one-up him, that somehow I was taking something away from him. He never said anything, but I felt bad about it."

I explained to Alex that twins often have a diminished capacity for enjoying their accomplishments because their gains highlight their twin's losses. Having grown up experiencing himself as part of a "we," it was no wonder that acknowledging or feeling proud of a singular success felt inauthentic and upsetting for him.

Given that Brad wanted to distance himself from Alex to find his own direction, I told Alex that he could seize this moment to pursue a change in himself. The personal transition from "we" to "me" would likely be difficult, even painful, but absolutely worthwhile. I assured Alex that he could challenge himself to develop a stronger sense of singularity and to honor the individual self that he had so often felt obliged to suppress.

Connecting to Oneself

Alex and I talked about managing triggers that arise in his relationship with his brother—for example, Brad's failure to give Alex the attention Alex craves, Brad's "unfeeling" responses to Alex, and Brad's ignoring of Alex. We discussed how, in these circumstances, Alex may feel compelled to be ingratiating to elicit a needed response from his brother. Instead, Alex could try to find strategies that will help him focus on being there for himself.

During our sessions, we talked about how Alex's sense of panic when Brad isn't there for him and his need to please Brad to manage that panic originated in his family. His parents were in constant turmoil, and there was so much tension in the family that no one could take care of him emotionally. In fact, Alex came to believe that taking care of his mother was his responsibility. As a child, he often felt helpless and powerless. So when he has that same feeling now, he gets triggered into that old state of panic. We discussed that Alex now can recognize that he is no longer helpless or powerless, that he has his own inner strength to handle the panic and anxiety. He can also learn not to get overly invested in taking care of other people but rather to concentrate on taking care of himself.

After many such discussions, it was a breakthrough when Alex reported to me, "When I can feel my heart beating or there's a pit in my stomach or I'm nauseous, I know that I'm overreacting to somebody else's feelings. So I try to take that feeling and put it outside of me. And I recognize that it's not my issue to deal with." Alex was beginning to recognize that the traumatic triggers are not about his own feelings and that he doesn't have to be responsible for his brother's feelings, his boyfriend's feelings, or those of any other person he interacts with. He can concentrate on his own inner feelings and not what he believes to be those of the other person.

Alex also told me, "I used to get so annoyed when I saw Brad acting in a way that was not really who he was. I have stopped putting energy into believing that I can read and know Brad's intentions. It's a waste of time and unproductive, and it's liberating not to do that anymore."

Believing that he could read his brother's intentions and feelings is what one would expect if Alex was merged with Brad. When one person feels merged as a twin, it is often the case that the twins are in the habit of reading each other nonverbally and are afraid to say or do anything that would cause the other person discomfort or anger. So when Alex initially disclosed that he could read Brad's intentions, it was because he felt like he knew Brad so well that he never had to ask his brother what he was thinking or feeling.

Because they grow up using nonverbal communication habits—reading facial cues and body language, for example—twins believe they have an ESP-like ability to know their twin as well as the twin knows himself or herself. Sadly, this prevents same-age siblings from authentically getting to know each other. They don't engage with each other to really learn who they are because they think they already know.

Also, because they are so focused on the other sibling, they very often don't get to know themselves.

In explaining what is lost when one engages in reading another's feelings or intentions, I talked to Alex about *self-states*. When Alex said he could tell that Brad wasn't being himself and that he wasn't acting like himself, I described self-states this way: "Brad was in a different self-state than what you were thinking he was in. When you believe that you know what your twin is thinking and feeling, you are essentially engaging in a one-dimensional way of thinking. In fact, we all have a number of different self-states, and our mental health is about integrating and accepting and understanding all our various self-states. So this feeling that you know your brother's intentionality without even having to speak with him means that you are neglecting to acknowledge all his other aspects—in other words, all his additional self-states. Being aware of the fact that every individual has a range of self-states is crucial if you are to truly understand other people—and yourself."

Alex's crisis of identity derived in part from his inability to acknowledge that his brother was more than what he intuitively "knew" about him. His process of individuation involved acknowledging Brad's various self-states and discovering Brad's distinct uniqueness. When Alex shared that he had stopped putting energy into believing that he could read Brad's intentions, it was an indication that he understands that although he may have thought he could read his brother's intentions, he really can't. The brothers are two people, and as often as they might intuitively know what the other is thinking, they *don't always know*. This epiphany signaled Alex's unmerging with Brad.

Another indication of Alex's burgeoning sense of singularity was in his relationships with boyfriends. He told me, "Until recently, every relationship I've ever been in . . . it's always about if the other person likes me. I could never say 'I'm not really into you that way' or 'I don't feel the same way about you.' If somebody liked me, I just let it happen. And then eventually it would just fizzle out."

I asked him, "How have you managed to let these relationships fizzle out?" And he said, "I don't really know."

Recently, however, Alex acted on his own behalf to prevent a potential romantic relationship that he did not want to get involved in. He told a friend who suddenly professed his love for him that he wasn't interested in anything romantic. Although Alex felt bad for hurting the guy's feelings, it was a breakthrough nonetheless. Rather than just let it happen as he always had before, he honored his own feelings and got up the nerve to express them.

Given his merged relationship with his twin brother and their fraught family history, Alex never felt separate enough to allow himself to figure out who he was and whom he wanted to be with and to be clear about his own feelings. He never articulated his feelings with his brother because he believed that they intuitively knew what the other was feeling. Being honest with the friend who wanted to become lovers was a positive indication that Alex is capable of expressing his true feelings, getting in touch with what he wants and needs, and discovering who he is as an individual.

Another big change, and a very positive one, occurred in one of our later sessions when Alex was able to say to me, "No, Joan, you're wrong." Throughout our time together, he had often responded to whatever I said with, "You're right." So when he told me that I was wrong in my assessment of a particular incident, I said, "Oh, thank you for telling me! I don't like being right all the time!" Alex began to feel entitled to express his particular ideas and opinions without fear or trepidation.

Leaving his abusive boyfriend at the same time that his brother was breaking away from him had led Alex to seek therapy. Desperately confronting loss and abandonment, he couldn't go to his brother to get solace or support, so that's when he started to see me. The challenge for

Alex was to become a new person, to not lose himself in the old feelings of being overwhelmed, helpless, and undeserving. I originally told Alex, "You have not had many opportunities to figure out who you are and to be proud and strong in your acknowledgment of that person. You have that chance now."

Alex is changing. He is getting acquainted with himself and with a new sense of authenticity. He is actively working on developing a singular self and trying to stay connected to it.

Disparaged Twin Identity

Now let's explore what can happen when parents insist that a third sibling be considered an integral part of the twinship dynamic.

Escalating tension between Darla and Doreen brought the thirty-four-year-old identical twin sisters to therapy. Their hostility toward each other had reached the point where they had recently gotten into a physical fight. They had often had verbal disputes but nothing this intense. What instigated the scuffle? It seems that Doreen tried to enter into a conversation Darla was having with a group of friends at a party. Darla was incensed that Doreen was trying to usurp her friends, so she shoved her away, and one shove led to another.

A number of issues were underlying the sisters' antipathy toward each other. Darla worked as an assistant to an event planner and was supporting Doreen, who was frustrated in her efforts to come up with a business plan and to design a website for an event-planning business the twins wanted to start. Darla was tired of Doreen not pulling her weight financially, and she was also losing patience with how long it was taking Doreen to finalize their business plan. She had been at it for several years already. Meanwhile, Doreen resented the fact that Darla didn't appreciate how hard she was trying to lay the groundwork for their new enterprise. They also fought over who was sacrificing the most in the caretaking of their older sister, Helena, who was living with them and having emotional problems. It seems that each was at the outer limits of tolerating the other.

When I inquired as to why it had taken so long to get the business plan and website completed, Doreen replied, "There are incredible barriers preventing regular people—especially women—from making a go of it. It's like the odds are stacked against us from the get-go."

Darla chimed in, "Most of the time, she's not even working on the project. She's too busy taking yoga classes and biking at the beach."

Visibly irate, Doreen said, "I'm the one who has to make sure Helena is doing okay! Taking her to yoga and biking is part of my unpaid job!"

Helena is two years older than Darla and Doreen. She is the only one of the three sisters with a college degree. She previously had a good job but has recently struggled to overcome severe bouts of depression. For the past year she has been living with Darla and Doreen because of their mother's directive that they look after Helena to make sure she's okay.

Growing up, the twins were given the unspoken message by both their parents, but especially their mother, that they were not to outshine Helena, who was not as attractive as the beautiful twin sisters. Although Helena was very smart, her mother felt bad for her because she wasn't pretty. Whenever Darla and Doreen were admired for being adorable twins, their mother became upset.

Darla recalled, "If we were at the mall with my mom and someone came up to us and said something like, 'What adorable twins!' my mom would pull us away without saying anything. We always were made to feel guilty about it, even though it wasn't our fault."

Their mother's defensive attitude on behalf of their older sister set up an emotional dynamic that was the opposite of what often occurs in families with twins. In many families, twins are put on a pedestal just for being twins, which creates an idealized identity based on being half of a special twosome. However, Darla and Doreen were ostracized by their parents simply for being adorable twins, and they were unfairly held responsible for their older sister's suffering. They received attention from relatives, children at school, and strangers at the mall for being a star package, but they got criticized for it by the two individuals whose opinions meant the most: their parents.

In high school, Darla and Doreen entered a talent contest as singer-songwriters, but their mother once again reprimanded them for making Helena feel slighted. Even though she earned higher grades than either of her younger sisters, Helena resented the fact that they got recognition and adulation from others at school.

In addition, their father's religious beliefs prompted him to call out the twins for being "prideful." He told them, "Calling attention to yourself and showing off is sinful." So their mother didn't want them to shine because their celebrity and popularity upset their sister, and their father believed that any attention they brought to themselves was morally wrong.

Despite their parents' lack of support, the sisters had begun to set goals for themselves, but they seemed unable to make much headway. Doreen tried to educate herself online about how to draw up a business plan but became easily frustrated. Darla was gaining experience in her job as an assistant to an event planner but hadn't gotten up the nerve to ask her boss for more responsibility. When a friend with the appropriate experience and connections offered to help them with the business plan, the sisters neglected to follow up. Although they both voiced their desire to make the event-planning business a reality, they weren't any further along in making that happen than they'd been three years ago.

Having grown up with the admonition that it was wrong to draw attention to themselves and to succeed as a duo, it was understandable that when they tried to develop a business together, the sisters unconsciously engaged in self-sabotage. Their lack of sufficient effort in pursuing their goal ensured their failure.

We talked about whether following through with their vision of owning their own business was somehow threatening to them. At first they denied that they were ambivalent about succeeding. "We both really want this to happen," Doreen said. "It's just that things haven't always gone our way." Darla added, "There's also the stress of dealing with Helena's depression, which definitely saps my energy."

I told Darla and Doreen, "Your family made you feel guilty, made you believe that it's wrong to highlight your strengths and to promote yourself. It seems to me that both of you have come to feel that it's wrong to succeed—that being successful will somehow be harmful to your sister. You have grown up believing that your duty is to think of her rather than consider your own needs—to be her caretakers rather than focus on developing your skills and planning your own future. This has been going on for years. So now, each of you has to decide if you really want to begin realizing your own full potential."

I turned to Doreen and said, "You'll have to learn to stick with this project, even if it's difficult and challenging. And if you really want this business to happen, you'll have to make a serious commitment to it and not worry about parental judgment."

I told them both, "If you're not interested in and committed to the project, then you each need to move on with other plans. You've been stuck for too long, and now you have to get unstuck. I'm sorry to be so hard on you—"

Darla interrupted: "No, we appreciate your honesty, Joan, and we really need a witness."

Doreen added, "This is what we needed to hear."

Darla's and Doreen's escalating hostility toward each other had signaled a crisis of identity. While they had good intentions—creating a business together—they couldn't seem to break out of the roles they had inhabited throughout their lives. Their family history had cast them as beleaguered twins who were obliged to never outshine their older sister.

Their role in life, their identity, was based on making certain that they didn't call attention to themselves. Failing to fulfill their personal vision was essentially an obligation. If they wanted to succeed, their sense of who they were meant to be—as individuals and as twin sisters—would need to be radically altered.

I think Darla and Doreen were grateful that I helped them elucidate their multifaceted conflicts. They were so lost amid all the pieces of their ongoing situation—their mother's condemnation and pressure to take care of their sister, their sister's depression, their father's religious pronouncements, and their frustration over their business plan never coming to fruition—that they couldn't seem to make a move. Their therapy provided a clarification of the sisters' experience that they didn't have access to before. In a relatively few sessions, they gained needed perspective: a narrative that resonated with the twins and made sense to both of them.

Having the opportunity to share their story with someone who could explain the likely causes of their hostility and self-sabotage—and articulate the relevant twin issues—energized Darla and Doreen, enabling them to commit to moving forward with their vision.

There's No Me without Her

It may be easy to understand how sharing a living space as well as the dream of creating a business together can result in friction. But what happens to twins with merged identities when they no longer live near each other?

In her early twenties, just out of college, Briana found me on the internet. She had recently moved to a new city where she didn't know anyone and started a new job, and she was anxious and depressed. "I don't know what I'm doing here," she said. "Actually, I don't even know who I am anymore. I feel like I've been plopped down in the middle of a foreign country where I don't belong."

Briana's twin sister, Faith, had used her connections to get Briana an entry-level job with a nonprofit organization, telling her it would be a good way for her to get her foot in the door. Briana told me, "I'm really not that interested in this kind of work, but Faith convinced me it would be a good move—and I trusted her. Now I think I'm regretting it."

I learned in our first session that Briana and her sister were always together growing up. Briana was "the follower" as she put it, and she believed that Faith was "basically better at everything." Faith was highly motivated and had no trouble deciding on a career path right out of college, but Briana didn't know what she wanted to do. She said she "kind of liked the idea" of working with young children and perhaps becoming a kindergarten teacher, but she wasn't confident that she could stand up in front of a classroom—even a classroom of five-year-olds—and be in charge. "I've never been the leader of anything," she said. So instead she went along with Faith's suggestion that she take this "great job that will be a fantastic opportunity for you." Witnessing her sister moving ahead with her own plans, Briana was desperate to find her way, so she agreed to move across the country and take the job. Once she was in her new apartment and at the new job, however, she quickly became overwhelmed.

Panicked over not knowing how to handle her new life, Briana contacted a therapist, who focused on her difficulty acclimating to the new job and strange city. "When I told her that I felt lost without my sister, she kind of brushed that off," Briana told me. "She just said, 'Well, it's perfectly normal to be homesick.'" That's when Briana searched for a twin specialist and found me.

During our first video chat, I asked Briana about her problems at work. She said that she had tried to figure out her responsibilities but couldn't really relate to the overall objectives that the group was working toward. And she felt that her coworkers were letting her know in not-so-subtle ways that she wasn't good enough. She didn't want to be there but felt that she had no choice. Her sister thought this was a great opportunity for her and had gone out of her way to get her the position, but now Briana felt desperate. She didn't know if she was going to be able to stick it out.

I asked her if she had talked to Faith about how things were going so far. She said, "We talk and text all the time, but, of course, she just tells me to hang in there. She doesn't get that I'm going crazy, and not having her here . . . I just don't feel like myself."

Until she separated from her sister, and until we talked about it, Briana had not been fully aware of how heavily dependent she was on Faith. In fact, she took all her cues from her sister and, in essence, sacrificed her own initiative. Now she was in a new situation: trying to cognitively face her struggles on her own. She hadn't realized how she allowed the twinship to rob her of the ability to figure out who she was and what she wanted. Rather than testing the waters by perhaps becoming a teacher's aide in a kindergarten classroom, she had already given up on the idea of working with children because she felt that she wasn't capable of becoming a teacher.

The more we explored the roots of her poor self-image, the more it became clear that ongoing comparisons to Faith were the overriding factor. Briana said, "In school, everyone expected me to be like Faith because we looked alike—but I could never, ever match her. I didn't make friends easily, so I basically relied on her for that. Everyone loved her. I played the guitar a little, and at one point I wanted to try writing songs. But Faith was already so good at it, why even bother? Same thing with the volleyball team—I didn't try out because I knew I probably wouldn't make it. I was an okay player but not a standout like Faith."

One thing Briana "achieved" that Faith didn't was developing an eating disorder in her junior year of high school. "Getting really thin was a way to feel good about myself," she said, "but Faith told me it was stupid, so I stopped." Even when it came to choosing healthier behavior, Briana needed Faith to lead the way.

Briana was envious of Faith's attributes and angry with herself for being so dependent and passive. She had no sense of herself apart from being Faith's "less-than" sidekick. She said that whenever she heard about Faith's achievements, she would feel worse about herself. In other words, she was constantly in comparison mode and had the sense that only one of them could be successful. And it was never she. Briana had no real sense of herself as a separate person; she had given over her power to her twin sister. Sadly, her self-definition was being Faith's appendage.

The therapy would need to focus on helping Briana develop the ability to push herself beyond the fear of being on her own so that she could handle risks and failure and catch up on the developmental milestones she had missed out on because she had been so crippled by her twin attachment. I wanted to help Briana understand her twinship issues and to feel more integrated and more positive about her own abilities.

I began our third session by posing a fundamental question: "What do you imagine your life would be like if you could give up the role of follower? What if you could forget about competing with Faith and become your own unique person? From what you have told me, you have spent a lifetime taking a backseat to your sister, which means you haven't had the chance to get in touch with yourself. Maybe you were afraid that if you were more assertive, you might alienate Faith and lose her protective guidance. Or maybe she was so dominating that you felt you couldn't even try to be assertive. What do you think it would take for you to jump out of that backseat?"

Briana teared up, and then she responded, "I always wanted to be like Faith. She's my twin, but she's an intellectual and an extrovert, and I'm neither of those things. I get so down on myself for not being more like her. But I want to stop being depressed—and I want to stop being so down on myself."

One of the first actions Briana decided to take was to curtail her lengthy phone chats with Faith. She confessed that she needed to set some boundaries because "Faith does all the talking anyway." Not having to pay as much attention to her sister's opinions and advice would be a good first step in separating from her.

We also explored the possibility of Briana's going to graduate school to pursue an education degree. She said it made her feel good just to think about doing something that was her idea and that fit her own interests and personality: "I love kids, so maybe I could make it work," she said.

Contemplating the issue of constantly comparing herself to Faith, Briana acknowledged that it would be a challenge to stay focused on her particular strengths and talents. I suggested that her new place of employment—although not the ideal situation—offered an opportunity to be seen as herself since no one there knew Faith.

In the following session, Briana reported that things had gone a bit better that week: "I decided to give up having a drink when I'm feeling down. I realized I'm not really an addictive personality anyway." Then she gave a half-smile and added, "Except I guess I'm kind of addicted to Faith—which I'm trying to give up, too." In fact, she had been talking and texting less frequently with Faith and was beginning to feel the difference between missing her sister and needing her. "Of course, I miss her," she said. "But maybe I don't need her to feel that I can make it on my own."

Now that she is considering the possibility of grad school, Briana is trying to adapt to her current work environment, knowing that it's a temporary situation. She has followed my advice and is appreciating that no one is comparing her to Faith. She's planning to stay at the job until she figures out her next move. Meanwhile, someone at work gave her a compliment for a task she had completed, and she was able to acknowledge to herself that she had indeed done a good job.

Overcoming the temptation to compare oneself to one's twin is a challenge many twins confront. Armed with a deeper understanding of the twin issues that held her back in establishing a singular identity, Briana is trying hard to develop and acknowledge her strengths and talents without making comparisons. She recently told me, "I guess we will always compare ourselves to each other, but I'm working on not believing that just because one of us is 'good' at something, the other doesn't have to be 'no good.'"

As Briana continues to make room for more self-defining behaviors, she is learning to let go of her "follower" role and to instead follow her own inclinations.

Crises of Identity: Variations on a Theme

Alex's crisis of identity was that he had to learn to define who he was without Brad's "conscience" and constant companionship. For Darla and Doreen, the challenge was to break free from the disparaged twin identity foisted upon them by their parents and older sister, who resented their "star package" attractiveness. And Briana had to overcome feelings of inadequacy when comparing herself to her twin sister, Faith, and to instead develop her own sense of self.

Each of these individuals, due to his or her particular twinship issues, had to begin the process of individuation somewhat later than most singletons. But crises of identity can happen at any point in a twin's lifetime. Such episodes may occur when twins in their late teens or early twenties separate after high school, go to separate colleges, or move away for a job; when one twin gets a life-threatening illness or dies; when one gets married or has children; or when one decides that he or she no longer wants to be as close to his or her twin and the other is emotionally left behind.

A woman in her sixties told me that she finally became so sick of never having established her own life due to her unhealthy attachment to her twin sister that she decided to get help to try to break her codependency with her sister.

A man in his forties came to see me in shock because his brother "just snapped" and told him "I hate being a twin." This man had organized his entire life around his belief that his twin attachment was absolutely wonderful, only to discover that his brother's anger and annoyance were the exact opposite of how he felt. He never had a clue his brother felt that way.

Such crises are often what bring twins to therapy, and a therapist who is knowledgeable about twinship issues can be of tremendous help. Often the event that triggers such a crisis can seem minor if the therapist is unaware of such issues. For example, one college-age client had what could be termed a crisis of identity the night she left her twin sister at a party. The sister was drunk and wanted my client to stay, but my client felt strongly that she needed to leave. When she got home, however, she was flooded with guilt and told herself, "I should have stayed to make sure my sister was okay." Getting in touch with her own needs and feeling righteously selfish triggered my client's intense panic and sense of guilt: "I felt like a terrible person and a terrible sister because I had left my sister at the party."

This triggering of guilt feelings happens a lot when twins are just beginning the process of individuation and learning to set boundaries and limits. They often have such transitional traumas because they are confused about when it is okay to take their own needs into account and move forward. In the case of the young woman who left her sister at the party, she was absolutely correct in honoring her own needs. Her crisis of identity led to a small step forward in her process of developing a sense of self.

Defining who we are as individuals can be a lifelong process. For same-age siblings, that process is interwoven with the connection one has forged with one's twin and the impact that connection has on one's singular identity.

CHAPTER 6

Replacement Twins

Given the defining role that twins often play in each other's lives, it is not unusual for adult twins to seek a twin-like relationship with a friend, lover, or significant other. Reaching out for a *replacement twin* may be due to an unconscious longing for the closeness that existed in the twinship, an unacknowledged desire to resolve unresolved issues between oneself and one's twin, or simply an inclination to continue being part of a dyad that in some way resembles one's relationship to one's twin. When one grows up with a twin as a primary partner and without a developed sense of self, finding a replacement twin to feel complete becomes an emotional necessity, even a compulsion.

Relationship problems between a twin and his or her friend or lover may involve excessive interdependency, caretaking/cared-for issues, or unrealistic expectations, which can often be traced to the twinship. Dealing with such issues in therapy necessitates a thorough exploration and understanding of the client's particular twin dynamic.

Losing the Connection Would Be Unbearable

Olivia and Spencer had been together for four years. During the previous six months of their relationship, they had lived in nearby cities due to their respective careers and got together on weekends. They'd had their ups and downs, but Olivia was unprepared for Spencer's bombshell announcement that he'd recently had a brief affair. Olivia told me this was "an unbelievable betrayal" since she had been faithful during their time apart. She called me in tears.

During our first session, Olivia explained how her relationship with Spencer began: "I met him my first semester in college, and I think I was obsessed with him immediately. I'm not even sure why, but the attraction was so strong. I'm not proud to admit it, but I neglected my studies somewhat because I was spending all my time at his place. He was a good student, so I can't blame him for my slacking off, but I let things slide because I was so into him. I cooked meals for him and looked forward to being with him whenever he wasn't busy studying. I remember my sister really came down on me for getting bad grades that first semester."

Olivia's sister, Jenna, was her twin, a fact that Olivia did not divulge right away. She mentioned that Jenna had begun to break away from her as soon as the two started college: "Jenna started hanging out with people she'd met in one of her classes or whatever, so we weren't spending that much time together." Shortly after that not-so-subtle split, Olivia got involved with Spencer.

When I asked her how her relationship with Spencer had affected Jenna, Olivia said, "I wasn't really talking to Jenna that much anymore. She was still the studious 'good girl'—we'd both been good girls in high school, but now that I had a boyfriend and was hanging out with him, she disapproved. She'd say, 'Hey, what's going on with you?' and I just couldn't stand her good-girl attitude. I was doing my own thing, and I was happy with Spencer."

According to Olivia, her relationship with Spencer was fine the first two years, but by the third year, she began to doubt his devotion to her: "Sometimes he wasn't available for me when I needed him to be, and he seemed so locked into his study routine that he wasn't that much fun anymore." From what she described, Olivia seemed to seesaw from feeling needy and wanting more attention to losing interest and wanting to break up with Spencer.

In the months leading up to Spencer's affair, Olivia had been confused about what she really wanted from him. At times she didn't want him to be her boyfriend anymore and wanted her own space; then she would feel ashamed that she was too dependent on him; then she would attempt to pull back. When he expressed to her that he didn't want her to be so needy, she felt abandoned.

During our subsequent session, I shared with Olivia that I thought a lot of her confusion about her relationship with Spencer may have to do with the fact that she had never really examined her relationship with Jenna. So we began to explore their twinship.

Olivia said that she had a tendency to feel bad about herself because "always being together with Jenna" throughout her childhood constantly brought up feelings of competition and comparison. She said she had always defined herself—her looks, her accomplishments, her moods—in terms of how she stacked up against her sister. And she confessed that she felt good about some aspect of herself only if she thought it was "better than Jenna": "I feel bad having these competitive feelings about Jenna because I love her and it makes me feel like a bad person. I don't want to feel good just because I'm better at something than she is, but it's just the way it is. When I met Spencer, he told me the reasons why he liked me and not Jenna—and that made me feel not only separate from her but really good because it proved I was better than her in one sense anyway."

Olivia revealed that in her family, she was always seen as the "angry twin." Jenna was much more even tempered and rarely got upset. Olivia didn't understand her anger and felt that it made her more of a bad person. It was one more reason for her to disapprove of herself, especially in comparison to Jenna.

I tried to help Olivia understand some of the underlying reasons for her anger. I said, "It makes perfect sense that you would be angry, given the fact that you perceive your sister as Miss Perfect and feel that you are in constant competition with her. No wonder that makes you angry. And given what you have told me about your family, neither you nor your sister grew up learning how to express anger. You weren't allowed to. Your parents appeared to be getting along all the time, so you had no role modeling for how to understand conflict or angry feelings. There was no safe place to talk about these very normal emotions. So being angry makes you feel like a bad person. But you're not a bad person. You're a person with legitimate feelings that need to be expressed."

It was helpful for Olivia to know that she could come to therapy and get angry, talk about having been angry about something, or express any other feelings she might have—and know that it was perfectly fine.

As we began to sort through Olivia's confused feelings about Spencer, it became clear that she had essentially replaced her twin relationship with the Spencer relationship. Because her relationship with Jenna had been fundamentally defined by comparison and competition, Olivia had little opportunity to figure out who she was apart from her sister. And at the moment that opportunity arose—as Jenna broke away from her in their first year of college—Olivia attached herself to Spencer. She didn't know who she was without being in a relationship.

The push-pull of wanting to be with Spencer and wanting to separate from him also mirrored her dependency on and need for separation from Jenna. As her initial attraction to Spencer began to fade, Olivia realized that they weren't that well suited to each other, but as she put it, she felt that "losing the connection would be unbearable."

And Spencer's affair brought up something else, in addition to a feeling of betrayal. The fact that Spencer would leave her for another woman brought back the old competitive feeling of not being as good as her twin. The infidelity crisis resonated in terms of Olivia and Spencer's unacknowledged replacement twinship. One of the only ways in which Olivia felt that she had something different from her sister—the only thing that set her apart in a positive way—was having a relationship with Spencer. Even though she knew that she had outgrown the relationship and that both of them needed to move on, the idea that she would lose the connection triggered her into feeling like the losing twin.

As Olivia came to acknowledge the link between her need to separate from Jenna and her attachment to her boyfriend, she was more motivated to make the break from Spencer. She said, "I've known for a long time that I needed to do this, but now it makes even more sense." She finally did just that. She still talks to Spencer and they are still friends, and Olivia is no longer tormented by the loss of their relationship.

Committed to striking out on her own, Olivia continues to struggle with anxiety issues; she knows, however, that anxiety is often an unavoidable piece of the individuation process. In one of our recent sessions, she said, "For now, I don't really want a relationship. I want to find myself and be engaged with things I like to do. I want to feel good about myself without that good feeling being connected in any way to feeling better than Jenna."

Forming a romantic relationship that is unconsciously based on competition with one's twin can have negative consequences. The same is true of close friendships, as the next case demonstrates.

Three's a Crowd

A professional woman in her early fifties, married with two adult children, Audrey came to see me with what she described as "an embarrassingly petty problem" that nonetheless seemed to be disrupting her life. Soft spoken and careful in her choice of words, she began our first session by saying "I know this shouldn't be upsetting me this much, and I can usually tolerate most difficult situations, but sometimes I feel so angry with this person. I can't express it or tell her why because, well, it would destroy everything."

"This person," Audrey explained, is her friend of thirty years, Jillian. The two have an unusually close relationship. They speak on the phone every day, have lunch or go on a hike together every Saturday, and often take vacations together. Their respective husbands don't seem to mind or to be threatened by the women's friendship.

The reason Audrey was so upset was that after she and Jillian had planned a trip to Hawaii, at the last minute Jillian announced she had invited a new friend of hers to come along. Audrey was very upset but didn't say anything to Jillian. She was withdrawn and quiet during the trip and had a horrible time. Noticing that Audrey was even more reserved than usual, Jillian confronted her about her demeanor after they returned home. Audrey couldn't bring herself to confess to Jillian why she was so hurt. So she used the excuse that she wasn't feeling all that well in Hawaii. But the upset feelings festered. Unable to control or process them, she contacted me.

I asked Audrey to describe her friendship with Jillian. She said, "We are so compatible—and we have so much fun together. Jillian always gets to know everyone and is extremely outgoing. When she's in a room, she fills it up with her wonderful energy. I just love being around her."

Audrey described herself as "quiet and shy" and Jillian as "funny and warm"—which Audrey loves about her. "I love that she draws people to her and is the life of every party," she said. "But the trip to Hawaii was supposed to be just the two of us, and the whole dynamic changed when it became a threesome."

I wondered if she'd had friendships in her past that had been as close as hers with Jillian, and Audrey said, "Well, I guess my twin sister." I asked her to talk about how her relationship was with her sister, and she said that, during their childhood, "she kind of took care of me in the sense that she would be the one to make friends at school and I would join in. Also, she stood up to our parents when there was an issue, allowing me to stay in the background and keep to myself. I guess I still tend to have that quiet nature."

I explored with Audrey how her relationship with her twin sister might be related to her friendship with Jillian. Although Jillian is not exactly like Annaliese, she serves a similar function. For one thing, Jillian eases Audrey's path socially. Because Jillian is someone who gets to know people easily, when Audrey is around Jillian, she doesn't have to put much effort into socializing; it's done for her. Since Audrey is shy, that works perfectly for her. And since she doesn't really want people's attention drawn to her, Jillian is a good partner because wherever they are, the attention is always drawn on Jillian.

On the other hand, Audrey is more emotionally nurturing than her friend, which appears to fit into Jillian's need to be mothered. Not only is Audrey a great listener, but she is always there with a pot of soup when Jillian is ill and more than willing to drive Jillian to doctors' appointments. Having been "overly mothered" by her twin sister, Audrey now dislikes that type of treatment from either her husband or friends. She said, "Annaliese was overprotective of me—which kind of drove me crazy. I had enough of Annaliese always wanting to help me when I was a kid, and now it turns me off if someone acts that way with me."

Instead Audrey likes to feel needed, and since Jillian is emotionally needy, they seem to be a perfect fit. Unlike in her twinship, Audrey feels that she's taking care of someone. So this thirty-year-long friendship is actually the reverse of her twinship. Audrey is the emotional caretaker for Jillian but without the competition that was always in play between her and Annaliese. And Jillian can serve the sociability function that Annaliese once served but without the attendant conflict.

Given the crucial roles that Jillian plays in Audrey's life—the social and warm yet needy friend—it makes sense that sharing her with a third person would present a serious conflict. I assured Audrey that feeling upset about the Hawaii trip was not a petty concern and that bringing the issue to the fore was a positive indication that she wanted to understand her feelings more deeply.

Knowing that the friendship with Jillian represents a more amenable twinship, Audrey can now think about how she may want to improve it. We talked about how twins often have a hard time sharing their feelings with each other because they are brought up with the unreal expectation that they are in perfect harmony and thus have little need to communicate on a deep level. And because Jillian is a kind of replacement twin, perhaps Audrey felt uneasy sharing her disappointment and hurt over the change of plans concerning the Hawaii trip.

I told Audrey, "If Jillian is the good friend you describe her as being, she likely will be able to hear what you have to say and understand your feelings, even if she doesn't share them. For instance, you might tell her that her sociability is something you love about her but that you were disappointed when she invited the other woman because you were expecting the Hawaii trip to be just the two of you. Allowing yourself to be open and honest with Jillian will most likely deepen, not endanger, your friendship."

I explained to Audrey that the next time she felt upset or hurt, she could choose to articulate how she felt before the situation became more troubling. Since she had little experience openly sharing feelings with her twin, it would not be easy to do so with her best friend at first. But it was important for Audrey to understand that telling her friend how she feels—even if she is angry over a perceived slight or transgression—would not "destroy everything." Although she may have grown up believing that twins should never fight for fear of breaking a sacred trust, close friendships, even those that might resemble a twinship, are not usually that fragile.

Dominated by His Brother, Then His Wife

In the above cases, interaction between the client's twin and replacement twin is a reenactment of earlier twin dynamics. But what happens when these two parties don't get along?

When Gabe came to see me, his presenting issue was that the two people he loved the most in the world were literally making him sick. Unable to sleep and battling stomach ailments and migraine headaches, he said he was completely run down by his unwanted role as "silent referee." His wife, Angela, and his twin brother, Chris, were each pressuring him to emotionally abandon the other.

Married for three years, Gabe had come to perceive himself as the middleman between his brother and his wife. Chris had never liked Angela, and the feeling was mutual. Gabe had kept up his relationship with Chris by getting together with him without Angela. He and his brother lived about thirty miles apart, and they saw each other about twice a month on a Saturday or Sunday. Chris dated off and on but didn't have a steady relationship, so he was usually free during the day on weekends. As for Angela, she was part of a large family, and she and Gabe spent much of their free time socializing with her relatives. Gabe enjoyed being with her brothers and sisters, but Angela never invited Chris to be part of their family gatherings. She seemed to be threatened by Gabe's close relationship with Chris. In fact, she frequently demeaned their "twin thing," as she referred to it. Gabe remarked that Angela would often tell him, "If you weren't so into your weird twin thing, you'd be more available on the weekends like a normal husband."

The situation came to a head when Angela glimpsed Gabe's phone while he was texting his brother and saw the phrase "your super-controlling wife . . . why is she such a bitch?" Angela became enraged and forbade Gabe from seeing Chris.

Of course Chris was furious and told his brother, "How can you put up with her? It's like you're living with a dictator!" Gabe had never been one to debate with his brother, so he failed to defend his relationship with his wife. But he told me that he was "seething" inside: "I hated Chris for criticizing Angela. I'm aware that her personality can be abrasive, and I think it's unfair for her to tell me I can't see my own brother, but I love her. And I love Chris—he's my best friend. I've just always hoped that by keeping the two separate, I could have a good relationship with both of them. Now I don't know what to do."

As I encouraged Gabe to talk about his relationship with Chris, he acknowledged that Angela was not the only one his brother had been critical of: "Chris is a great guy, but he can be harsh. There've been times when he's made some pretty judgmental comments about the women he's dating. And I guess growing up he was kind of bossy with me. But it was usually in a helpful way."

Like many twins, Gabe was reticent to discuss any disagreements he'd had with his brother. But when the subject of Chris's tendency to be judgmental or bossy arose, I brought up the similarities between Gabe's relationship with Chris and Gabe's relationship with Angela. Gabe had never fully acknowledged the dynamic between him and his brother—how he had always accepted Chris's domineering ways. And not until the flareup between Chris and Angela brought him to therapy did Gabe begin to perceive the similarity between how they each related to him. "It's true that Angela kind of lovingly takes charge, and I'm okay with that," he said. "And I guess that's how Chris is sometimes, too. So maybe I'm used to it."

We discussed the fact that because Chris had been the more dominant twin, that dynamic seemed perfectly normal to Gabe, which is why his relationship with his wife feels familiar and generally acceptable. I explored with Gabe how Angela might be perceived as a kind of replacement twin—someone who could "lovingly take charge" and whom he could lovingly go along with. Only when the two people he loved the most clashed did problems arise.

But to what extent did Gabe want to continue being dominated—by either his wife or his brother? During our sessions together, Gabe revealed a repertoire of rationalizations for Angela's controlling behavior: "She likes things to run smoothly; she grew up in a large family where you had to be forceful to be heard; she's a strong woman, and I respect her for that." It seemed that Gabe played an enabling role in their passive/dominant dynamic by always siding with Angela. When I brought this up, Gabe confessed that he wished he had the ability to call her on some of her more abrasive behavior, but, he said, "I feel burdened by having negative feelings for someone that I love so much."

I shared with Gabe why twins so often have trouble acknowledging any negative feelings about or differences of opinion with their same-age siblings: "Twins are very often brought up with the notion that they are each other's perfect partner and that they will always be emotionally in sync and never be in conflict. Believing this, they can find it traumatic to disagree with their twin because disagreeing means they're not connected. Unfortunately, this is why articulating your own needs or wants becomes so difficult—because it might invite conflict."

I told Gabe that the goal is to accept the fact that you can be in conflict with your brother—or your wife—over various issues and at the same time accept and appreciate the many positive aspects of your relationship. Neither reality has to negate the other. My analysis seemed to resonate with Gabe, although he seemed troubled by its implications. He said, "I've always tried so hard to avoid conflict, and I always thought that was a good thing. It's what my dad was so adept at."

He then brought up the fact that he thought he was a lot like his father: "My mom was the live wire and my dad was the quiet one. But they loved each other. I think my dad knew how to keep the peace by going along with my mom sometimes, even when he didn't necessarily agree with her. I guess I take after him."

His father's temperament and relationship with his mother likely had a significant impact on Gabe, but the twinship dynamic was probably an even greater factor. And Gabe was beginning to understand that. Chris had always been the dominant twin, and Gabe had been okay with that, just as he had generally been okay with Angela's dominance—until it resulted in her decree that he cut ties with Chris. Gabe cared deeply for both his wife and his brother and had not wanted to lose the connection to either of them by advocating for his own needs. But his physical symptoms had sent the signal that he needed to change the way he related to the two people he loved the most in the world.

Armed with a new understanding of how his relationship with Angela was a reflection of his twinship, Gabe came to realize that he didn't have to make himself sick by allowing either his wife or his brother to control his life. Learning to gradually relinquish the submissive role that had always felt so comfortable to him would be a challenge. But if he wanted to rid himself of the physical and emotional distress he had been experiencing lately, he could no longer afford to play the passive middleman.

Replacing Her with Him

As many of the case histories in this book have revealed, adult twins who have failed to adequately develop a sense of self share a kind of fused identity with their same-age sibling. When one twin finally separates from the other for whatever reason, the "left behind" twin no longer has someone with whom to share that identity. And without someone else to whom they are connected in this way, the abandoned twin no longer knows who he or she is. One common scenario occurs when one twin marries and the single twin hastily follows suit. As Sandbank points out,

> After the first twin marries, or forms a new partnership, the second may find a partner quite quickly, even too quickly, but some may need time to work through their feelings and find a new identity.[1]

Leanne's story closely mirrors that scenario. She and her sister, Maggie, are thirty-one-year-old fraternal twins. When Maggie announced that she was marrying Peter, her boyfriend of several years, Leanne feigned enthusiasm. She threw herself into helping Maggie plan the wedding, choose her dress, and organize a "wild bachelorette party." But the frenzy of wedding preparations barely masked Leanne's panic. She would later tell me, "Maggie getting married was like a death to me—the death of her and me."

Six months after her sister's wedding, Leanne came to see me. Her presenting issue concerned her boyfriend, Jason, who happened to be her brother-in-law's best friend. Leanne said, "I knew Jason before the wedding, but we started hanging out after Maggie got married. He's great, and it's cool doing stuff with Maggie and Peter, but I guess I don't think he's really for me. And now I don't know how to get myself out of the relationship."

When we delved further into her concerns, Leanne told me she's not sexually compatible with Jason, and they don't have much in common other than the fact that he is closely connected to Maggie through Peter. She said, "At first it seemed like a perfect match for me. But unless we're hanging out with Maggie and Peter, I'm not really that into him."

Before exploring her dilemma surrounding Jason, I asked Leanne to tell me about her relationship with Maggie. She replied, "We've always been a team. It's not that we agree on everything or have exactly the same tastes or personalities, but we just fit together perfectly. She's got my back and I've got hers. I don't have to explain myself or hold back. Maggie accepts me completely for the crazy person that I am."

When I wondered what she meant by "crazy," Leanne added, "I guess I have a sort of wild side to me and Maggie gets that. She doesn't look down on me for it. When we were little, I made her laugh a lot with goofy stuff I did. In high school, even if I got in trouble for doing weird pranks or whatever, she stood by me— even with our parents."

Although Leanne had indeed panicked when she realized that her sister's marriage would open a new chapter in Maggie's life, she could not let go of the hope that her relationship with her twin would remain unchanged. I explained to Leanne that perhaps the reason for her panic was that her very identity as half of the Leanne-Maggie "team" was in jeopardy, meaning that Leanne would have to cultivate a new identity that did not include her sister. I suggested that perhaps in an effort to postpone the inevitable, she had chosen a boyfriend who would not only ensure her ongoing connection to Maggie but also might be able to function as the Maggie part of a new team.

In fact, as I learned more about her relationship with Jason, we discussed the similarities between her connection to him and the roles she and Maggie played in the twinship. For example, Jason was often the appreciative audience to Leanne's gregarious, "crazy" personality, in much the same way that Maggie had been. And he seemed to accept her for who she was, without trying to change her in any way. But Jason wasn't Maggie, and although Leanne acknowledged that Maggie would remain a loving presence in her life regardless of her marital status, the era of the twin sisters as a duo had passed. And Leanne was sadly aware of that seismic shift in the sisters' relationship.

When she later admitted that characterizing that shift as a death was "probably overly dramatic," I assured her that her statement contained an emotional truth. Being forced to emotionally separate from her sister due to Maggie's marriage likely felt overwhelming to Leanne, as it ushered in a sense of profound loss. Not only was she losing the dynamic of closeness she had always had with her sister, but she now found herself on the brink of having to more fully define herself as an individual.

In our discussion of her relationship with Jason, I shared with Leanne that her rush to become involved with him was likely related to another issue as well: competition, something that twins constantly confront. Perhaps her drive to connect with Jason so quickly after the wedding reflected her desire to be on a similar timetable as Maggie with regard to finding a mate. While singleton siblings may also be aware of how closely they follow a brother's or sister's various milestones—settling on a career, getting married, having children, buying a house, and so on—twins are even more compelled to make comparisons. Was it possible that Leanne didn't want to be out of sync with her twin when it came to finding a partner?

Leanne was silent for a few moments and then responded, "I don't know. Maybe you're right. When we were little, we used to say that when we got older and got married, we'd live next door to each other and our husbands would be best friends. But it was always just kind of a silly fantasy. And marriage wasn't something I necessarily looked forward to. My relationships with men have always been more casual."

Leanne then expressed her fear that perhaps, unlike Maggie, she didn't really need or want a serious boyfriend or a husband: "We've both had boyfriends off and on, but I never felt like I needed to get really close to anyone—because I had Maggie. Now that she's got a husband, I don't know where I stand with her . . . or what I want from a lover."

As I have counseled many twins over the years, I told Leanne that for twins who have a particularly devoted and loving connection, accepting that no other relationship will be equal to their twinship can be difficult. However, expecting the same type of connection with a friend, lover, or spouse is unrealistic. Same-age siblings share a unique personal history, and their friendship is often—although not necessarily—uniquely close. So measuring other friendships or romantic relationships against what one has experienced with one's twin is unreasonable. Every relationship has its own distinctive qualities, strengths, and flaws.

Whether Leanne latched on to Jason with the ulterior motive of staying connected to the newly married couple or with the unacknowledged hope that her new relationship would replace the closeness she enjoyed with Maggie, I assured her that coming to the realization that she did not want to be Jason's girlfriend was a good sign. It meant that she was getting in touch with her authentic feelings.

Acknowledging that she did not want an intimate relationship with Jason, as well as understanding some of the reasons why she may have connected with him in the first place, was an important step. So was accepting the fact that her relationship with Maggie had reached a new stage, one that required Leanne to become less attached to her sister.

The goal now is for Leanne to develop and feel comfortable with a singular identity—without depending on a twin sister teammate or a surrogate twin boyfriend to complete her. Focusing on herself and getting to know herself better before heading into another relationship will be a challenge. But clarifying her twinship issues in therapy was an excellent beginning. With a stronger sense of self, Leanne will likely be prepared to make wiser choices regarding her next intimate relationship. Once she feels ready to become seriously involved with someone, she will be able to do so without the need to forge a twin-like connection.

Replacement Issues

The case studies in this chapter highlight only a few of the issues that clients may bring to therapy with regard to twin-like relationships or replacement twins. As I pointed out in my previous book *The Same but Different*, a twin's struggles within a relationship can sometimes be traced to the unconscious need to replicate the twinship in some way.[2] For example, if the twin dynamic was defined by dependency and that issue is not addressed, a similar dependent situation may arise in a twin's relationships with close friends or romantic partners. If a twin was the caretaker to her same-age sibling, she might seek someone with whom she can continue to fill that role—or she might shun serious relationships to avoid such caretaking. If the twinship was a particularly close one, one or both twins might expect a level of closeness with best friends or lovers, only to become disappointed when that closeness doesn't materialize.

In my practice, I have come across these and other replacement twin scenarios:

- Being accustomed to the effortless rapport with his twin, a client has his expectation dashed when a friend or partner doesn't understand him in a similarly effortless manner.
- Believing that twins should always get along, a client habitually avoids conflict by adapting to the needs of a twin-like friend or lover—and consequently fails to get her needs met.
- Having filled either the cared-for or caretaker role with his twin, a client chooses friends or lovers who will replicate the opposite twin-like role, only to be disappointed when the relationship dynamic somehow breaks down.
- Avoiding friendships for fear they may be too intrusive, a client fails to acknowledge that the avoidance is rooted in her having been intruded upon by her overly needy twin.

The key to dealing with all these issues is to help clients develop a stronger sense of self so that they have the capacity to enter into and enjoy relationships on their own terms, free of twin-related psychological baggage. With a strong sense of their own inner strengths, inner capacities, and inner resiliency, clients are then able to navigate challenges without resorting to a replacement twin.

CHAPTER 7

Significant Other versus Twin

Depending on the nature of the twin attachment and the degree to which each twin has developed a singular self, a number of conflicts may arise involving same-age siblings and their significant others. For those whose twinships are exceptionally close, disappointment and distress may occur when a marriage or romantic relationship fails to mirror the same level of connectedness. For twins who feel differently about maintaining a close attachment, a relationship with a significant other can bring those differences to light. And partners or spouses may have issues of their own: some resent having to compete with a twin for the love and attention of their significant other, while others may use their partner's twinship as an excuse to avoid emotional intimacy. Throughout my practice, I have found that the "significant other versus twin" issues clients bring to therapy are as distinct as the individuals and couples involved.

Erecting New Boundaries

"I love my brother," TJ told me, "but it's gotten to the point that he's seriously interfering in our family and adversely affecting my marriage. I really don't want to have to choose between him and Gail, but she's had it with him."

The crisis between TJ and his identical twin brother, Todd, arose due to a disagreement over how TJ and his wife, Gail, were handling their new role as parents to their infant son. Like other first-time parents, the couple read many of the current parenting books on how best to manage a baby's sleep routine, and they decided that picking up the baby when he cries at night, feeding him, and letting him sleep in their bed was working out for all three of them. But a fourth person felt the need to weigh in: Todd. He and his wife had two young children and, according to TJ, "Todd considers himself a baby expert—in fact, he considers himself an expert on a lot of things." At a recent family gathering, Todd had come on so strong with Gail, arguing with her about their decision to let the baby sleep with them, that Gail was nearly driven to tears.

TJ explained, "He really lit into her, and Gail is not someone who enjoys an argument, so she just kind of let him say his piece. But afterward, she was really upset. She told me that night that she doesn't want to be around him anymore. I felt bad that she had taken the brunt of his argument because I was in another room at the time. But on the other hand, I'm so used to Todd's over-the-top way of expressing himself that I figured Gail could just let it go."

When I asked TJ to describe his relationship with Todd growing up, he said that his twin had always been somewhat controlling but he was used to it and it never really bothered him. Unlike his boisterous, opinionated brother, TJ was mild-mannered, and like his wife, he tended to avoid conflict. So TJ's way of managing the twinship was to passively accept his brother's domineering behavior.

TJ said, "Sometimes Todd spoke for both of us, even though there often were times when I disagreed with what he was saying. But it just seemed pointless to voice my opinion because he was louder and more forceful. So I'd just let it pass. I knew in my mind that I was my own person, even if it didn't seem that way to other people."

TJ also said that when he met Gail, he felt that he had found someone whose sensibility closely matched his: "Even when we don't agree, we're able to talk about things without getting so dramatic or angry like Todd. We're both even-tempered and handle things in a pretty calm manner."

TJ loves Todd and doesn't want to lose their friendship. He wants to continue to include his brother in his life without it being an emotional burden for Gail. I told TJ that maybe it was time for him to be more honest with Todd about the consequences of his controlling behavior. TJ said that for the first time in his life, he wanted to do exactly that, which was why he had come to therapy to validate his plan to "have a talk with Todd."

We talked about TJ's newfound desire to call his brother on his off-putting behavior, and I asked him, "Do you think your new identity as a parent trumps your previously passive role in the twinship? Because it appears to me that for the first time, you are willing not to simply let it go but to stand up for your own ideas and values."

TJ agreed with my assessment. I validated his recognition that it was perfectly understandable for him to want to call out his brother on his intrusive behavior. Under the guise of being helpful, Todd had intruded in TJ's life and the way he and his wife were choosing to parent their child. I told TJ that Todd didn't have the right to tell either of them that what they were doing was wrong. Although TJ had never bothered to confront his twin before, he now felt compelled to do so.

During our next session, which took place after TJ and Todd met to discuss Todd's outburst at the party, TJ said that Todd had a hard time accepting what he had to tell him. But TJ held firm in his commitment to level with his brother about respecting the boundaries between the twinship and TJ and Gail's marriage. He said, "When I told Todd that it was our business how we choose to raise our son, he became defensive—and kind of nasty. He wanted to know why Gail hadn't stood up for herself at the party and why I had to be her mouthpiece. I let him know that

Gail is not someone who enjoys arguing and that she and I are absolutely on the same page when it comes to our son's sleeping habits. I told him that the point is, he simply can't interfere in our decision-making and he has to respect my relationship with Gail."

We talked about the fact that it may take some time for Todd to adjust not only to the new boundaries being established between the brothers but to TJ's forthrightness. I told TJ, "It's quite likely that Todd has always felt he could get away with controlling you. And since Gail holds a similar anticonflictual stance—one that you are now willing to abandon—he probably felt that she was an easy target as well. Once it sinks in that you and he are on a more equal footing and that you are willing to stand up for your values and beliefs, perhaps Todd will relinquish his attempts to bully you with his controlling behavior. In either case, it is to your credit that you have overcome an old twinship pattern."

Interestingly, TJ is a much more accomplished person than his brother, but he had always taken the path of least resistance because he didn't want to deal with Todd's overpowering behavior. At this stage in TJ's life, however, his new identity as a parent is overriding his passive twin identity. No longer willing to go along with his brother to avoid conflict, TJ is firm in his resolve not to let the twin connection dictate his parenting decisions or his marital relationship.

We Long for Validation from Our Husbands

In response to a blog I wrote about conflicts between significant others and twins, I received this message on my website from Sophie:

> I would love to find out more information about how to determine what my twin sister and I can do to work through our similar issues with our husbands. We both have a sense that we are taken for granted.
>
> We are both giving people yet have an awareness of how to be independent and make ourselves happy. Somehow we both long for validation from our husbands. In the past we have felt that our

husbands use the excuse that they can't make us happy because what we really need is a twin. We both feel this is unfair and not the case. We do talk on the phone often to share what is going on in our lives and get the affirmations that we long for . . . which helps.

We are wondering if we need to learn something about our twinness or if this is due to how we were raised or if it's something we need to develop within ourselves.

In our first video consultation, I asked Sophie to tell me about her upbringing and the nature of her relationship with her twin sister, Grace. She told me that as teenagers, the two were professional athletes who competed in the same sport. They were coached by their father, who always encouraged them to support each other; he taught them not to think of competing against each other but rather to focus on doing their personal best. Sophie said, "He told us that if we held the mind-set of competing against each other, we would never be happy. He said that we should be happy if we do well, but we should also be happy if our sister does well. So if I had a bad day and Grace had a good day, we both were happy that one of us was successful."

I remarked that her father's advice was commendable and that it had likely contributed to the sisters' close, supportive relationship. Sophie added that growing up, the girls shared a very good friend but they each had their own girlfriends as well. They rarely fought, were each other's best friend, and lived together after leaving home until Sophie got married and moved to a different city.

Grace married about six years later. During the years that she was single, she missed Sophie's companionship but used the time on her own to develop new skills and interests. Sophie claimed that Grace had managed to strengthen her sense of individuality during that time; however, she also said, "Grace told me that if she had been the one to find love first, she's not sure she would have been able to leave me. If that had been the case, though, I hope that I would have had the love and strength to encourage her the same way she supported me. We have always wanted each other to experience great things individually. The thought of holding each other back from all the happiness and experiences that life offers would feel just as uncomfortable as leaving. It's not what being a twin is about."

From what Sophie revealed, it was clear that her relationship with Grace was exceptionally supportive and loving. While their attachment was emotionally very close, they were aware of the need to cultivate their individuality.

With regard to the predicament concerning their husbands, which was what had prompted Sophie to contact me, it was interesting that they had very similar dilemmas: they both claimed that their husbands were not giving them the validation and loving attention they desired. In our next session, Sophie and I explored the nature of her marital relationship. She began by telling me, "I had always assumed that when I married and had kids, the connection to my husband would be like the connection I had with my twin." Instead, her relationship to her husband more closely resembled her connection to her father, who was trustworthy and loyal, as well as forceful and independent.

When Sophie described her husband, it was in the context of both her own marriage and Grace's: "Both of us married very strong, independent men who aren't really into sharing feelings. My 'aha moment' was when I realized that we had both unconsciously chosen this type of person because of our father—he had literally and figuratively 'managed' us, and we unquestioningly followed his advice. Still, I held out hope that my husband would soften and become more of a soul mate."

I remarked to Sophie that what had been so attractive to the sisters when they fell in love with their respective mates—that the men were strong and independent—was now presenting a struggle. Sophie's recognition that the girls' father had been a positive role model who had influenced their choice in men was significant. The sisters were proud of their athletic achievements, and Sophie acknowledged that their coach-dad had played a key role in their success. She and Grace respected and loved their father and in fact credited him with instilling their need to support rather than compete with each other. But Sophie's "hope" that her husband—who shared certain key qualities with her dad—would radically change from the strong, independent guy he was to the twin-like partner she envisioned was unrealistic.

We talked about why it was unreasonable for Sophie to expect to duplicate with her husband the intimacy and shorthand communication that she shares with her sister. I explained that many twins who have enjoyed a close, loving relationship with their same-age sibling set the bar too high when it comes to what they expect from a significant other, only to be deeply disappointed. I used as an example an incident that Sophie had related that caused her to get her feelings hurt and to resent her husband: "You mentioned that your feelings were hurt when your husband took off on Saturday to go mountain biking without asking you to join him—even though he knew you wanted to go, too. And that he often goes off on his own or with a friend on Saturdays. But maybe he enjoys doing certain things without you. That doesn't necessarily mean that he is 'devaluing' you, as you contend. It simply points to a difference in how the two of you define and experience togetherness."

Contributing to the discord between Sophie and her husband was her accusation that he uses her close connection to Grace as a reason to denigrate the sisters' bond: "My sister and I use words of affirmation to show our love for each other. But our husbands both seem to withhold that kind of support—because they think that is what they call 'a twin need'... and they think we just need to 'grow out of it.'"

I agreed with Sophie that her husband's remark sounded defensive. His contention that her need to hear "words of affirmation" is something she should "grow out of" is unfair. Regardless of one's age or level of maturity, it is perfectly reasonable to want to receive a supportive, kind word from a loved one. What Sophie's husband may have been reacting to was her not-so-subtle directive that he show his love and support for her in the exact same way that her sister demonstrates those things.

We talked about how singleton spouses or partners sometimes perceive the twin connection as an impingement and an intrusion, which can make them feel vulnerable and anxious to the point that they may need to defend themselves against it—as Sophie's husband had done with his defensive remarks.

How could Sophie deal with the disparity between her expectations and her husband's behavior? I suggested that first, she needs to find activities that she enjoys doing either by herself or with friends so that she won't be so dependent on her husband's attention for her sense of well-being. Also, rather than trying to make her husband demonstrate his love for her in a way that she's used to experiencing with her twin sister, Sophie can tune into and learn to accept the unique ways in which her husband shows her that he cares. Perhaps, too, she can pull back from trying to constantly please her husband—which, given his independent nature, he may perceive as a smothering kind of love. Her need to do so may be related to her and Grace's need to please their coach-dad to gain his approval and love.

In one of Sophie's final email messages to me, she expressed her gratitude for our being able to openly discuss and appreciate the unique connection between twins—and how it differs from a loving connection between her and her husband:

> Most people don't understand "connection" the way my sister and I do. . . . I have come to understand that it would be unfair for me to expect a singleton (my husband) to know what it's like to have a deep sense of connection without the feeling of the independence being threatened. There is a beauty in a healthy twin relationship that cannot be put into words.

Overinvolved Twin, Angry Husband

In chapter 1, I referred to Claire who was taken by surprise when her husband accused her of damaging their relationship by being overly involved with her twin sister, Rebecca. A crisis ensued when Claire invited Rebecca to stay in their guesthouse for a few weeks while she looked for a place of her own. Rebecca had just broken up with the boyfriend with whom she had been living and had also recently lost her job. For Claire, "it was second nature" to be caring toward her sister and to help her out. She didn't understand why her husband, Ted, would have a problem with that.

Married only a few years, Ted and Claire found me on the internet after Ted read my book on adult twins and gave it to Claire in the hopes that she might gain some insight into her relationship with Rebecca. In my initial session with them, Claire told me that Ted had become so enraged with Rebecca that he was no longer allowing her in their home. According to Claire, the altercation between Ted and Rebecca was over a relatively minor incident, but it proved to be the last straw.

"It all started over nothing, really," she said. "Ted and I came home from the movies one night and Rebecca was watching TV. There's a small TV in the guesthouse, but she was in the main house watching the larger set. There were some snacks on the coffee table and a few empty bottles—not that big of a deal. But Ted flew into a rage, telling Rebecca he'd had enough—that this was our home, that she had worn out her welcome, and that she needed to find her own place immediately. Rebecca was crushed, of course, and I felt absolutely horrible."

Ted laid down the law: not only was Rebecca no longer welcome in their home, but Claire shouldn't see her anymore if she wanted to preserve their marriage. He defended his decision: "I love my wife, and I don't want her to be unhappy, but I need her to respect the fact that our home is our home—not her sister's. Rebecca disrupts what Claire and I have together. It's better for everyone if those two keep their distance."

Claire said she was so distressed over Ted's demand that she cut off contact with her sister that she started drinking a lot, which in turn made Ted even more upset with her. At the time of our session, Claire was no longer drinking and was going to Alcoholics Anonymous, but she hoped that the therapy would give her more insight into her relationship with her sister and help her deal with Ted's negative feelings toward Rebecca.

Claire said she was very sad and upset that because Ted refused to be around Rebecca, they would not be having Thanksgiving dinner with her extended family as they usually did but would be celebrating the holiday alone.

I asked Claire to describe her relationship with Rebecca, and she replied that they were "naturally very close, as most twins are." When I pressed her for more details, she said, "I guess over the years I've worried about her a lot. She's had a harder time than I have when it comes to relationships and getting her life together. She was married briefly, but the guy was no good. And the boyfriends she's had since then haven't treated her that well. She deserves so much better. I've always been there for her to talk to, and I'm more than happy to do that—but Ted thinks I'm too involved in her life. He thinks that having a few phone calls with her every day is way too much. But it's normal for me to check in with her often to find out how things are going. Texting isn't enough. I want to hear her voice."

Ted countered that he didn't think calling your sister twice a day every day was "normal" and that the sisters' relationship got on his nerves. He also said, "Rebecca has a very aggressive personality—especially with me."

Claire acknowledged that Rebecca can be "overly assertive" at times and that this had precipitated arguments with Ted prior to the incident that led to her being banned from their home. According to Claire, Ted has a tendency to be very dogmatic, so his clashes with Rebecca were inevitable. "They both have strong personalities," she said.

Another factor in Claire and Ted's marital difficulties was that Ted often accused Claire of taking Rebecca's side rather than his. Claire said that she is only trying to mediate between the two and that she doesn't think of herself as taking sides. What she wants more than anything is for Rebecca and Ted to get along. But Ted felt that Claire was not living up to her role as his partner.

Claire explained the situation from her perspective: "Even if I tell him something like, 'Well, maybe what Rebecca meant by that was…' or 'Maybe Rebecca was just trying to…' he'll come back and say, 'No, don't stand up for her. You're my wife and you're supposed to be on my side.'"

"She's right, I do need her to be on my side," Ted said, "and that's how it should be."

I suggested to Claire that Ted's need to have her "take his side" may be related to his family history. Ted had shared that he had been in therapy to try to work through issues related to his lack of appropriate parenting: "My folks were never really available, sort of in their own little world. It was the seventies, and they were living their version of the hippie lifestyle. I was too young to have a say or give my consent, but I was swept up in it."

So it made sense that Ted needed Claire to demonstrate that she was consistently available to him and that he could depend on her loyalty and love. At the same time, Claire needed Ted to accept her ongoing connection to her sister.

I posed this question to the two of them and asked them to think about their particular emotional response: "How would each of you have to shift your perspective for Claire to be able to spend time with Rebecca and for Ted to feel comfortable and secure enough to know that doing so was not an abandonment of him?"

In the next few sessions, I attempted to normalize the situation, to let both Claire and Ted know that spouses married to a twin may feel that their role as the significant other is being usurped by their mate's twin. Claire didn't realize that she was as attached to her sister as she was because for her, being closely connected was the norm. She didn't think anything was weird or wrong about checking in with Rebecca twice a day, and she couldn't understand her husband's perspective because, as I reminded her, she and her sister had always lived in a twin bubble. Prior to Claire's marriage to Ted, both sisters were happy with things as they were, so they had no need to change their dynamic.

Until the blowup after Rebecca moved in with them, Claire had not been aware of how impacted Ted was by the twinship. When they had quarreled about Rebecca in the past, Claire's attitude had essentially been "This is just how we are. Why do you even care? How I am with my sister is completely separate from you."

But Claire had to understand that the significant other who is feeling left out or in second place will not readily accept his wife's word that her relationship with her sister doesn't take precedence over their marriage when it appears to him that it does. Although Claire didn't think of Rebecca as being more important to her than her husband, she needed to realize that this was how Ted felt, and she had to figure out a way to let him know she was there for him while maintaining a connection to her sister.

As for Ted, during the therapy, he learned that making room for Claire's relationship with Rebecca could strengthen their marriage, rather than drive a wedge through it. Knowing how much the connection meant to Claire, his support would bring the couple closer together. We also dealt with Ted's history of feeling abandoned by his parents and how that influenced his relationship with Claire. Never having received the level of nurturing that he needed as a child, he had looked to Claire to provide that. And when her allegiance seemed to be to her sister and not to him, it triggered those childhood issues.

Claire also wanted to have a session that included Rebecca to let her know that while Claire was committed to improving her relationship with Ted, she still loved and cared about Rebecca. She was worried that her loving connection to her sister was in jeopardy. In the session with Rebecca, Claire began by saying "I know how upset you are. You've lost your job and your boyfriend, and you need my emotional support. And I want you to know I'm always there for you. I was more than happy to have you stay in the guesthouse temporarily. But I also have to consider Ted."

Rebecca nodded but looked very sad. Claire moved closer to her and gave her a hug. After a few moments, I added, "Obviously, Claire loves you very much and values your deep connection. But she has a different life now, and her marriage is her priority. So as difficult as it may be to accept, your relationship with each other won't be exactly the same as it was when you were growing up. Your lives have taken different paths."

Rebecca talked about how, as adults, the sisters had not had a hard time being independent and leading separate lives. Only when the boyfriend and job crises hit did she assume that Claire could focus on her and "not worry so much about Ted." I explained that while taking care of each other may have been an integral part of their twinship process when they were growing up, that dynamic is no longer viable. The sisters can still be close and loving, but they have their own lives now, and significant relationships with other people often take precedence.

It was not easy for either sister to talk about committing to a new chapter in their relationship, but both assured the other that they would continue to see each other, even if it involved some changes.

Several months after our initial meeting, Claire and Ted were getting along better. Claire was seeing Rebecca again but on different terms. With the exception of major family gatherings, the sisters were getting together on their own. Ted still didn't want to be around Rebecca very often, but he was amenable to Claire seeing her one on one. Claire found a way to reframe her relationship with Rebecca so that it wasn't so threatening to Ted and wouldn't make him feel abandoned and alienated. So a "new normal" was instigated whereby the sister connection was preserved and the couple's marriage strengthened.

Compromise is not always perfectly balanced or easy for the parties involved, but Ted and Claire were each able to get some of what they wanted. Claire is getting time with her sister, and Ted is being freed from feeling like a third wheel. And they can now attend next year's Thanksgiving dinner with the entire family, including Rebecca.

Dating a Twin Stifled by Stockholm Syndrome

Karen, a young professional woman in her midthirties, contacted me via the internet. She said she had an urgent need to speak with a psychotherapist specializing in twin issues as she recently had been romantically involved with an identical twin and needed validation that her assessment of his relationship with his brother was accurate.

What Karen relayed to me was a profoundly sad scenario. When she met Will, his twin brother, Ray, was out of the country. Will explained to Karen that he and his brother had never been separated for more than a few weeks. They lived together in a house owned by their parents and worked together in a family business. Although such a relationship seemed quite unusual to Karen, she ignored whatever doubts she may have had. "I was very attracted to him, and we seemed to have a lot in common," she said. "The twin thing didn't fully register. Or maybe I didn't want it to."

During Ray's absence, Karen and Will spent nearly every evening and weekend together. Barely one month into the relationship, they told each other that they were in love and even talked about having a future together. While Karen said that things were not perfect, she felt as if she had found the man with whom she wanted to spend the rest of her life.

Then Ray returned after three months of working abroad. Karen said that almost immediately, she felt an undeniable shift in Will's demeanor. His behavior as well as his emotional availability changed drastically. She gave an example: "If Will and I made plans to see a movie or play together, he had to check with Ray first to make sure that Ray didn't want to see it with Will. If he did, then Will and I had to choose something else. There was no apology or anything—as if checking in with your brother about where to go with your girlfriend was perfectly normal. I couldn't believe it. I guess I was so shocked I didn't quite know what to say."

Karen also noticed that Will now seemed extremely anxious whenever they were together. She said, "The only time he seemed to be able to relax was during sex. But now there seemed to be much less time to be together because he was so concerned about Ray—when they were getting together, plans they had made, dates that Will had to keep open for Ray."

On one occasion, Will and Karen were returning from a weekend holiday and were on their way to have dinner with Ray, who had set up the dinner plans before the couple left on their trip. Will and Karen were running late due to traffic when Ray called and berated them for not being at the restaurant on time. Karen said that Will was so distraught over his brother's rage that he drove recklessly at high speeds until they arrived at the restaurant. "We were only about twenty minutes late, but Ray barely even acknowledged me when we got there," Karen said, "and he was really snide to Will—acting as if we had committed a major crime."

Karen described the following scenario as a metaphorical illustration of her status in the triad: She purchased a small bag of chocolates for Will one day as a token of her affection and thoughtfulness. She told me that the bag of sweets lay on the twins' kitchen countertop for days. It was not touched, moved, eaten, or thrown away. She is convinced that Ray did not permit Will to do anything with the sweets other than have them lie there as a symbolic reminder that Will's relationship with Karen would not be opened, savored, or experienced. Their connection would be suspended and denied.

I told Karen that, from what she described, it seemed Will felt compelled to please his twin brother and do everything in his power to satisfy his brother's needs, and that not doing so terrified him. One could almost say that he was suffering from what is commonly known as Stockholm syndrome—a psychological state in which hostages become sympathetic to their kidnappers to survive. The term was coined after it was determined that hostages in a 1973 Swedish bank heist had formed a positive relationship with their captors. In a sense, Will had been psychically kidnapped by Ray, dutifully complying with the demands and obligations imposed by his dictatorial brother.

Karen was indeed accurate in her assessment that these two brothers were grossly interdependent in an extremely unhealthy way and that it would be unwise for her to stay involved with Will. She said that she had attempted to broach some of her concerns with Will, but he became defensive when she tactfully alluded to his being controlled by his twin brother. Will was unwilling to discuss Karen's concerns or observations. She eventually realized that the man she had thought she was in love with had no mind of his own when he was around his brother. I told her that she was fortunate to have had the emotional wherewithal to break up with him.

Since I did not treat Will or his brother, it is not clear to me how their twin enmeshment became so pervasive and pernicious; however, I am glad that Karen did not waste any more time feeling as if she could or should do something to change their dynamic. I told her that I appreciated the opportunity to validate her sensible response to her ex-boyfriend's unhealthy attachment.

A Confusion of Roles

A number of clients have told me that because of their close relationship with their twin, they feel as if they are second parents to their twin's children—that they are more closely related to their nieces and nephews than a mere aunt or uncle would be. Such was the case with Tina, Emma's twin sister. Emma didn't seem to mind that her sister felt like a second mom to her two young children; however, Emma's wife, Paulina, became incensed over a situation involving Tina babysitting their kids. It was at the height of that situation that the couple came to see me.

Emma and Paulina had been married three years. Their son and daughter were four and two years old. For several years, Tina had been their babysitter on Saturday nights, when the couple enjoy their ongoing "date nights." Tina is single and schedules her social life around her Saturday nights with her niece and nephew.

Emma explained how the babysitting routine got started: "Tina adores our kids. She's been closely involved with them from day one. In fact, she was as excited as we were when Paulina and I decided to become parents. As much as we love being moms, though, we both value our time alone as a couple, so our Saturday nights became sacrosanct. And it was a relief not to have to second-guess how our kids were going to adapt to a babysitter—they love Tina."

The conflict that brought Emma and Paulina to therapy centered on the fact that Tina had begun to bring her boyfriend with her on Saturday nights. At first, Paulina didn't say anything about the boyfriend, believing it was just a one-time thing. After he showed up with Tina a third time, Paulina confronted Emma. She didn't get a good feeling about the boyfriend and also doubted that Tina could fully concentrate on the kids when he was there. Emma said that she trusted Tina but was finding it very difficult to deal with Paulina's mounting anger. She felt conflicted about telling her sister she couldn't bring her boyfriend and guilty about being caught in the middle. In response to Paulina's pressure to confront her sister, Emma had a talk with Tina. She said, "I told her that Paulina would prefer it if she came by herself rather than with her boyfriend and that I had to respect Paulina's wishes as she was also the mother of our kids. Tina got upset and said that she was just as much a mother to them as Paulina. She said, 'You and I share the same genes. They relate to me like I'm their mom, too, and I feel like their mom. How could she think that I would ever do anything to harm those kids?'"

Paulina became visibly upset as Emma recounted her conversation with Tina. She said, "How dare Tina bring up the whole 'same genes' argument! And she's not the mother of our children. She's their aunt, period."

Nonetheless, Emma was understandably overwhelmed. She needed help to understand that her primary obligation was to her wife and the children they were raising, even though it meant that she had to risk upsetting her sister by telling her not to bring her boyfriend on Saturday evenings. I told Emma that by placing the blame on Paulina for having reservations about the boyfriend, Emma was inadvertently escalating the rift between her sister and her wife.

Also, I asked Emma to consider these questions: Was she perhaps ignoring a potential risk to her children by trusting Tina's judgment about her boyfriend? Was it possible that Paulina's intuition about the boyfriend had some validity? And was Emma so used to avoiding conflict with Tina that she might be turning a blind eye to the boyfriend situation? I encouraged Emma to think about the need to set boundaries and say no to Tina when that was the appropriate thing to do and then to learn how to accept her sister's being angry with her.

As for Paulina, I tried to explain to her what it's like to grow up as a twin. I thought she needed to try to understand from her wife's perspective how hard it is to say no to a twin because of the dynamic that they had growing up. I told her that from an early age, twins are accustomed to taking care of and looking out for each other—to a much greater extent than are different-age siblings. Paulina had very little awareness or compassion about the conflict and struggle her wife was going through. So helping her understand the ramifications of the twin connection and how it impacted her marriage to Emma was a valuable piece of the couple's therapy.

Conflicting Attachments

Given that twins inhabit a unique psychological reality and grow up closely attached to their same-age sibling, their relationship to a romantic partner is likely to be affected by that attachment. The case histories in this chapter attest to some of the varied issues that may arise.

Like Sophie and Grace, some twins may find their marital relationship deficient because of an unrealistic comparison to their twinship. And their spouses may understandably protest that there's no way they can ever live up to a twin's unique expectation of closeness.

In cases where one or both twins have not become fully individuated, competition with the significant other for the partnered twin's love and loyalty is common. Karen's unfortunate entanglement with her boyfriend and his controlling twin brother was an extreme example; Will and Ray's twin enmeshment meant that a significant other would not even be tolerated.

Very often, entrenched twinship roles are no longer acceptable to a twin or a twin's partner once they are in a primary relationship, as evidenced in TJ and Todd's story. Although TJ had previously accepted Todd's dominant role in the twinship, becoming a father and a husband provided him with motivation to change that dynamic.

Regardless of the particular issues involved, in most twinships a reassessment and redefinition of the twinship naturally occurs when one sibling marries or becomes involved with a significant other.

In their study "Twinship and Marriage—Experiences during the Course of Twin Relationships," Swedish researchers Sirpa Pietilä, Pia Bülow, and Anita Björklund found that while marriage can be a challenge for twins and their spouses, the twinship can also be a "resource" for the relationship. They also point out that the most successful marriages in their study involved spouses who were supportive of the twinship:

> In accordance with attachment theory and how twins are likely to regard each other as an attachment figure, the combination of

twinship and marriage seem to be a challenge for the spouse to be most of all. But when the marriage works, the twinship might be a resource rather than a risk to the marital relationship.[1]

In the harmonious marriages, the spouses were sympathetic and accepting of the twin relationship. . . . In difficult times the twin relationship served as a source of comfort and support.[2]

Despite the varying issues highlighted in this chapter, one interesting theme that emerges in nearly every story is that twins are surprised that their spouse or romantic partner doesn't understand how closely connected they are to their same-age sibling. Many twins seem unable to recognize that their closeness might be construed as strange, inappropriate, or disloyal to the significant other. It often does not even occur to a twin that wanting to routinely be with or at least check in with one's twin could be considered unusual. Even in the extreme case of Will and Ray, in which Will somewhat blindly goes along with what Ray wants him to do, Will doesn't seem to believe that being connected to his brother in this way is inappropriate or unusual.

The inability to relinquish a primary connection to one's twin originates in the twins' early attachment and their experiences growing up. Those experiences organize the twins' belief system, their expectations of themselves with regard to their twin, and their twin's expectations of them. For some twins, their same-age sibling is the most important person in their life. And it is important to acknowledge that nothing is inherently unhealthy or wrong in twins feeling that they are closer to their twin than to anyone else, including their significant other. If that sense of closeness is shared by both siblings and accepted by their respective partners, it is perfectly okay that the most "significant" person in each twin's life is the other twin.

In some cases, those who choose to be involved with a twin have an understanding that their partner will be more closely connected to their same-age sibling than to them. And they are fine with that. They may even feel that having a sister- or brother-in-law who is always there for their spouse takes some of the communication burden off of them. They may think that their spouse's twinship gets them off the hook of having to communicate on a deep level. As one talk-show guest confessed to me during a radio program:, "I don't have to open up that much with my wife because she has her sister for that." And his wife added, "My husband never complains about my relationship with my twin sister. He's not at all threatened, and he likes the fact that she and I are always talking and intimate. I'm happy in my marriage—and grateful to have my twin as my confidante."

This woman's husband, for whatever reason, did not find the twinship connection threatening, and he was happy that his wife had an intimate relationship with her sister.

We know that some people who are married to twins are perfectly comfortable with their marriage and with the relationship that their spouse has with his or her sibling. They may even appreciate the fact that their mate has a twin with whom to share his or her deepest feelings. Such people would not be contacting me, however, because they would have no problems or issues to work through.

But such acceptance of a mate's closeness to a same-age sibling is not always the case. Sometimes a person will fall in love with a twin and include the other twin socially at first. Maybe the singleton partner initially accepts the idea of the other twin being included in the couple's social life, and it doesn't seem like a big deal. However, in such cases, the partner may assume that incorporating the other twin into the couple's life is temporary and will not extend into their married life. He or she may not realize that a threesome relationship that begins when the couple is dating is likely to continue.

For example, a young man I met at a workshop was dating a twin and related to the group that when he and his girlfriend go out, her twin comes along. "She even travels with us on weekend vacations," he said, "and I don't mind." I told him, "This may seem fine now, but you have to understand that by accepting this situation, you are becoming involved not only with your girlfriend but with her sister as well." This young man didn't understand that. At this early point in the relationship, he seemed to enjoy the narcissistic thrill of being with two women who look alike. He disclosed that they had told him, "We're soul mates; we like going out together." But I don't think he had thought about the long-term ramifications of that statement. Perhaps, like many others who become involved with a twin, he assumed that should he and this young woman decide to get married, the sisters would be fine letting go of their togetherness.

As has been reflected throughout the book, the twin dynamic is as varied as the population of twins. And the conflicts and rivalries that can arise concerning twins and their significant others are likewise diverse. Having a therapist who is sensitive to and knowledgeable about twinship issues offers twins, as well as those in a relationship with a twin, the opportunity to work through problems of conflicting loyalties, relationship boundaries, and the potential transition from one significant other to another.

CHAPTER 8

Being a Twin's Therapist

When a twin tells his therapist that he feels abandoned by his same-age sibling who has a new girlfriend, enraged by his brother's intrusiveness but ashamed to admit it, or guilty for deciding to start a business without his twin, how does a therapist respond? One with little understanding or training in twin psychology might wonder: "Why is it such a big deal that his brother has a girlfriend? Why is he so ashamed of being angry toward his twin? Why does he believe he would be harming his brother simply by making his own business decision?"

Therapists who are unfamiliar with twinship issues would not understand that such concerns are characteristically magnified for a twin. They might not expect that a twin patient would enter therapy by presenting such exaggerated feelings about seemingly mundane situations or that a twin's reaction to a particular circumstance involving a same-age sibling is vastly different than a singleton's.

Sophie, whose story was highlighted in chapter 7, had seen several therapists prior to coming to see me. She sent me this email toward the end of our time together:

> Although those therapists were well intentioned, it took me years to realize that being a twin adds an element that most therapists don't know they should take into account when giving advice. Twins have experience with connection from the time of conception. It

can almost be like a marriage, where taking the other's feelings into account benefits the self. By the time twins are adults, they have had many more years with this experience than a singleton, which can make it even more difficult to navigate a world independently. I believe twins have the potential to long for a connection with others like we have with our sibling. However, therapists may see this as an unhealthy codependency when in reality it is a feeling of acceptance that is very special.

When therapists don't understand this special relationship that twins have, there is the potential that the advice that's being given does not make the patient feel understood. Therapists assume that twins know what it's like to be a singleton. For years I questioned if something was wrong with me, until I finally realized that my experience as a twin was unique from what my therapists understood. Thank goodness I found you . . . after years of not understanding . . . I finally was validated. Therapists don't know what they don't know.

A fundamental objective in being a twin's therapist is to validate the twin's experience. Given that our culture romanticizes twins and expects their relationship to be seamlessly harmonious, many same-age siblings grow up expecting that as well. So they are often afraid to acknowledge that problems exist or to communicate those problems to their twin. When they seek help from a therapist, they hope that the professional will understand the uniqueness of a twinship and the particular issues that can arise. When a therapist who understands the psychology of twinship articulates for a client what is actually going on between her and her sibling, the client not only feels validated but is relieved to finally gain clarity with regard to a defining aspect of her identity.

Being a twin's therapist is about helping same-age siblings see each other as people—apart from their role as twins. This awakening or discovery can be compared to young people finally being able to see their parents as people, rather than as Mom and Dad.

A twin's therapist can also help the client uncover twin-related issues embedded in conflicts that may not seem directly connected to the twinship. For a twin, having a therapist who is aware of why shame, anger, guilt, or anxiety may have roots in a twin's relationship to a same-age sibling—and who can empathically articulate those linkages—can profoundly enhance the therapeutic experience.

In this chapter I offer some of the core concepts and experiences that have shaped my own practice as a twin therapist, in the hopes that they will deepen your understanding of twinship issues and inspire your interest in treating twins.

My Therapy

The first time I saw a therapist, I was in my twenties. The therapy was required for my psychoanalytic training, as I was in the process of getting my first doctorate. I saw an analyst four times a week for four years, and my twinship never came up. My analyst knew that I had a twin sister, but the subject of our relationship was never broached. At the time, I was unaware of the impact my twinship had on the psychological issues I was confronting, so, of course, I never brought it up myself. Still, the therapist obviously didn't consider this core piece of my family history to be psychologically significant.

More than a decade later, I sought a therapist because I was completely overwhelmed by my hectic life. I was in the process of getting my second doctorate, writing my dissertation, taking care of my five children (ages six to fourteen), and struggling with issues involving both my husband and my twin sister. I was trying to balance many things at once, and although I had always been able to stay in control of everything, all of a sudden I wasn't the competent caretaker that I thought I was. Inundated and unable to keep everything running smoothly, I was trying to find enough time for myself, my kids, and my husband—and feeling like none of us were getting what we needed.

During the initial sessions with my therapist, we established that I identified as a caretaking person and yet I felt like I was not being the perfect caretaker that I considered myself to be—and that was causing me great anxiety. I had always prided myself on being an exceptional caretaker because as a child and a young adult, I had overseen the emotional well-being of both my mother and my twin sister. In fact, those experiences had been influential in my deciding to become a therapist. So when I began my therapy, I was at a loss to understand, "Why isn't this working anymore? Why am I having such a hard time being a caretaker to everyone?"

Although I was writing a dissertation about twinship issues, I had never really discussed my own twinship with a therapist. Judging myself to be an inadequate caretaker brought up for me the caretaking role I'd had with my twin, a role I had always been so good at. Sometimes in therapy, I would be associating to a problem or feeling I was having and would say something to my therapist like, "I think that has a lot to do with the twinship." Given that she was essentially unaware of twin psychology at that point, she didn't understand how a particular issue we were discussing related to my being a twin. I would explain the connection to her and she would, of course, be very interested in my input. For example, I would spontaneously make an association such as, "I think that whole situation really got exacerbated by being a twin," and she would respond, "That's really interesting. I never thought about that. That makes so much sense."

So in the course of my therapy, I taught my therapist about twinship issues. I related to her my experiences as a twin and why I felt that my twinship had influenced particular struggles I was going through. Also, since I was in the midst of writing my dissertation, my academic work informed my therapy—and my therapist—as well. As my therapist came to perceive the deficit of self that I had as a result of my family history,

I contributed to that assessment by bringing in the dynamics of my twinship.

The caretaking piece was very important. I had always been a caretaker, and not being able to be an efficient one when I came to therapy was a major concern. When I told my therapist, "I was the caretaking twin," and she asked, "What's that?" I explained that often in a twinship, if the mother or father isn't available, the twins are forced to take care of each other. So I was the caretaking twin, and my sister was the more vulnerable one whom I had to protect. As we got older, my sister became annoyed by and upset with my caretaking of her, which in turn made me feel sad and guilty. But I was still a caretaker.

I went on to play the caretaking role with my college roommate—a kind of replacement twin. Throughout my life, being a caretaker had defined who I was. It was a way to save myself because I felt valuable and important. I fell apart when I was no longer able to succeed in that defining role—and I needed a therapist to help me understand what was going on.

Sharing my insights relative to being a twin enabled my therapist to help me work through various issues that I had with my parents, my husband, and my twin sister. She of course knew about the caretaking dynamic—but not in the context of a twinship. Had I not been able to describe to her some of the basic elements of twin psychology, she would not have known how being a twin related to my deficit of self.

Over the course of my therapy, I learned a great deal more about the impact of my twinship from the person whom I had introduced to the subject. For example, I remember talking to her about the fact that my sister and I had different perspectives on childrearing, which at the time was causing me some distress. My therapist helped me work through why it was so difficult for me to acknowledge differences between me and my sister, and it was profoundly eye-opening because I had always assumed that we were alike in so many ways. I had been blind to how different we actually are. My burgeoning recognition of our differences came about in my therapy, thanks to the insights that my therapist provided.

And thanks to our long therapeutic relationship, the deficit of self that she so wisely assessed when we first met has increasingly diminished.

Relationality and Co-construction

When I began my career, I had classical Freudian training, as well as an introduction to self psychology. Neither of these models felt appropriate for the way I wanted to practice therapy. I was inclined toward what came to be known as *two-person therapy*, which is why I later embraced the *relationality* perspective. The relationality sensibility acknowledges that there are two people in the room—patient and therapist—who are always in a bidirectional, mutually influencing, and co-constructing system. In this model, in addition to thinking about and being present for the patient, the therapist is also thinking about herself, her feelings, and her own experience—allowing it to become a real part of what she brings to the therapeutic process. Perhaps this made more sense to me than classical theory because I'm a twin. The "self with other" model in relationality is certainly what spoke to me in understanding twinship.

Co-construction means that the two people in the room co-create meaning together. It is a theoretical term used to differentiate this type of therapeutic process from the one-person models originating with Sigmund Freud and Heinz Kohut, in which the therapist removes herself from the patient's experience. Freud's objective observer stance removed him from the patient; Kohut's existence as a separate yet related person precluded his entering into the perspective of the patient. Thus, while both theories are distinct, both maintain a one-person vision.

In the Freudian and self psychology models, the therapist constructs meaning from what the patient is saying, but that meaning does not utilize the full experience of the therapist. In the two-person co-construction model, the therapist adds her own experience to the therapeutic process and becomes a person in her own right. The hierarchical vision of the patient and therapist dyad in the one-person models is revised by embracing the notion of two people essentially on the same plane.

The premise that the therapist and patient are always co-creating meaning made sense and appealed to me. For me, employing co-construction with my clients is essential. It enables me to put everything about myself that feels relevant into the therapy. Inevitably, I bring in my mood on that day, my history, my feelings about the patient, and my parental and marital experiences. Everything about my life, external and internal, is in that room in that moment with the patient.

With relationality, meaning is derived during the therapy session from everything that has to do with the therapist, from everything that has to do with the patient, and from their interaction. This idea goes beyond the archaic notion that the awareness and life of the therapist are irrelevant. Rather, the therapy takes place in the moment and incorporates everything that both the therapist and the patient bring to the session. The therapist is no longer a blank slate; she is taken into account and responsible for what she is thinking and feeling. The therapy is thus fully a two-party dyadic model.

In relationality, the therapist has the option to self-disclose. The rule is that self-disclosure must always be done in the best interest of the patient and in service of the process. So, for example, if the patient senses something about you during a session, such as, "You look like you're really distracted and you're not really paying attention," the therapist might self-disclose by responding "Oh, I didn't realize that. Let me think about it." Being a twin, I might choose to self-disclose with a response such as, "I can understand that; I felt like that with my sister."

I believe that self-disclosing is simply being real. If you use it with the intent to benefit your patient or foster closeness between the two of you, it can be effective. However, it can also backfire if your patient feels that you are intruding on him with your own issues. For example, a client might say (or think), "Why are you bothering me with your issues? I don't want to hear this!" So it's up to you to weigh the advantages and risks and up to the patient to respond.

Mutual Recognition

Healthy relationships and twinships involve mutual recognition: each person in a dyad or a twinship acknowledges the personhood of the other. The other is perceived as a person in his or her own right with intentions, goals, interests, and feelings that are important to that person and do not threaten an intimate other.

With twins, the problem is that maintaining and achieving mutual recognition can be challenging. Nonindividuated twins define themselves in relation to the other. Often they perceive themselves as one person. If they cannot recognize their separateness, mutual recognition becomes impossible. They see themselves either as part of a whole or in opposition to another. Hence, they co-create a seesaw dynamic: If I'm up, you're down; if you succeed, I fail. One must be the winner; the other, the loser. Unable to recognize that the other is a person in his or her own right, the twinship becomes a dyadic complication working against the ability of the twins to appreciate and recognize each other as separate beings.

Sometimes a pair achieves mutual recognition, but then that achievement is lost and must be won again. This may result in an ongoing state of tension for some people. With twins, the situation can be more problematic. Those who have not been able to individuate as children continue to define themselves in relationship to the other. Since they perceive themselves as sharing an identity or being half of a whole, one is always the near opposite of the other. The achievement of mutual recognition is never lasting; it is constantly lost and regained.

The following is an example of how we might see the presence of mutual recognition—or the lack of it—play out in a twinship: One twin is getting married. Her sister has never been married and is not involved in a relationship. In fact, being in a relationship and getting married seem like unobtainable goals to her. The unmarried twin loves her sister and wants the best for her, but she is in conflict because she is also sad, envious, and fearful of abandonment. What might she say when it is her turn to give the wedding toast?

If the twinship involves mutual recognition and the unmarried twin can accept that she is in conflict over her soon-to-be married sibling's new status, she can lovingly wish her sister and brother-in-law the best while also acknowledging in her conscious mind (to herself) her sense of loss and jealousy. She might give a wedding toast that sounds something like this:

> I could not be happier for my sister, whom I love beyond words. Of course I'll miss our sisterly outings and daily chats, but I'm so happy knowing she is off on a wonderful new journey with my new brother-in-law!

Conveying with sincerity her best wishes while publicly acknowledging some of her conflicted feelings and acknowledging to herself the sadness and envy, she is able to be truthful to her entire set of emotions. In other words, she is able to *hold the conflict.*

On the other hand, a twin whose twinship does not include mutual recognition and who is unable to accept her conflicted feelings or to fully acknowledge her negative emotions would deliver a different wedding toast. Her negative thoughts would be dissociated—out of her awareness and unformulated. She may consciously do her best to behave appropriately; however, if dissociated painful feelings are outside her awareness, she might make a toast that goes something like this:

> I wish only the best for my sister, and of course I'm happy for her. Not so happy for myself, though. Miserable, in fact. But today it's all about my sister—so let's toast the happy couple!

Both unmarried twins love their married sister and want the best for her, and both have conflicted feelings. The difference is that the twin in the second scenario is involved in an *enactment*. Unable to hold conflict, she can't help but act out—and blurt out—her negative feelings. Thus, the dissociated feeling is publicly revealed.

Self-States

In relationality, the concept of a single self is rejected in favor of the concept of multiple selves. As Philip Bromberg says, health is feeling like one self while actually being many selves.[1]

We each carry within us multiple selves that emerge in different circumstances as various *self-states*. What is essential to a healthy perspective is to be able to feel like one self in a particular circumstance while knowing we have many self-states. So the twin in the first scenario can be in a "happy for my sister" self-state while acknowledging another self-state to herself: that she is going through some tough challenges surrounding her sister's marriage. Without that knowledge or ability to see ourselves in multiple ways, we cannot understand our own intentions and affects.

This is a key concept in treating twins because, due to their self-definition as being dependent upon and limited by how they are seen in the context of the twinship, they are often unable to perceive that they have multiple selves—that they are more than simply the opposite or mirror image of their twin. This notion of "If you win, I lose"—often referred to by Jessica Benjamin as a *doer-done to dynamic*—that one sees in breakdowns of mutual recognition organizes a twin's life so that he feels that his identity is based on either winning or losing, on how particular traits are dissimilar from his twin's, and on how he stacks up when compared to his same-age sibling.[2] The ongoing comparison to his twin, which denies the complexity inherent in every human being, profoundly inhibits the development of a separate self—not to mention a separate sense of self that includes an awareness of other self-states.

Thus, therapists need to be aware of the psychological handicap that many twins are burdened with by not being able to experience either mutual recognition or multiple self-states.

Twin Mirroring versus Parental Mirroring

In chapter 1, we discussed the importance of child-parent attachment and how that process may be overlooked by harried parents of two same-age babies. Too often, this attachment is displaced by twins' attaching to each other. Psychotherapist and twin Susan Fisher, in her article entitled "The Metaphor of Twinship in Personality Development," refers to "twin preoccupation" or twin mirroring and implies how it differs from the mother-child mirroring experience:

> What could be called "twin preoccupation" supplies a mirroring, narcissistic object which can be relied on for love and affection. The need for mirror acceptance and approval from another persists with lessening urgency throughout life. When a twin fills the need-satisfying role too well, there is not the frustration and gradual disillusion necessary for separation.
>
> The twinship inhibits real progress and commitment and creates a stalemate. Available energy tends to go towards preserving equilibrium with the twin at the cost of individuation.[3]

Nothing is more crucial to a twin's future individuation than a secure attachment to her parent. When a child is connected to her parent, the parent sometimes says yes and sometimes says no. The parent sets limits, and that is how the child learns to tolerate frustration, accept that she can't get what she wants all the time, and know that not everything she does is wonderful. Those limits allow the child to sometimes become angry and upset with the mirroring object (the parent) who supplies love but also frustrates her, gets angry with her, and doesn't always do what she wants. The child thus learns that she is not in control of the parent.

She must learn to deal with the fact that the parent both loves her and sometimes says no, which then allows her to separate.

Twins who primarily mirror each other do not have the experience of learning from an adult who loves and teaches them to separate in this way. Because their relationship with the parent isn't developed enough and is superimposed by their twin relationship, saying no to each other is merely a way of maintaining equilibrium between them. There is no overarching lesson that leads to healthy individuation because twins don't learn complete autonomous selfhood from each other the way a child learns from a parent.

As we discussed in chapter 1, twins whose primary attachment is to each other do not have the benefit of an attachment to a parent who can help them identify, articulate, and fulfill their needs. This often results in twins growing up and denying or being unaware of their own needs because they have been so focused on the needs of their twin.

Winnicott pointed out the profound difference between parental mirroring and twin mirroring by referring to the notion of looking *into* a mirror versus *at* a mirror. A child looks into the mirror when he *looks into* his mother's eyes and sees himself. The child learns who and what he is as a separate individual and as separate from his mother. When a twin *looks at* the eyes of his twin, he sees his twin but not necessarily the eyes of a separate other. He is merely looking *at* his sibling, not *into* him.[4]

Common Themes in Twin Therapy

In my twenty-five years as a twin therapist, a number of themes have emerged, all of which I have helped clients explore and many of which I have personally confronted. The following are some common themes that therapists treating twins need to be aware of.

Upbringing

Very often, twins are not fully aware of how their upbringing with regard to the twinship may have affected them as children and as adults. For example, Did their parents spend alone time with each one when they were very young? Did they ever engage in separate activities? Were they in separate classrooms? Did they go to separate colleges? Did they have their own friends at school or did they share friends? Twins who are not seen or treated as individuals by their parents, extended family, and others in their social environment have a tougher time developing a sense of self. Also, if as young children they were more attached to each other than to their parent, they are likely less equipped to separate from each other and to claim an individual self.

Separation and Guilt
Separation from one's twin can usher in a sense of freedom but also feelings of guilt for abandoning the sibling. The mix of emotions can be extremely frightening. The therapist must allow the patient to take baby steps, rather than expect her to embrace freedom right away. When one twin wants distance and separation, the other may feel tremendous resentment and betrayal. This expectable reaction can make the one who desires separation feel guilty, even ashamed. An internal battle may rage within her: Whom do I please, my twin or myself?

Separation and Panic
Separating from one's twin can be as fraught as separating from one's primary caregiver as a young child. If individuation does not occur in childhood, the process of separating from a twin can cause intense fear and panic. As Vivienne Lewin points out,

> The experience of separation from the twin may be of the same order of upset as a separation from mother. However, while the awareness of separateness and the process of separation from mother is part of a developmental process, separation from a twin is not an automatic process. Where there is a lack of individual development in one or both twins this may lead to a crippling twinship that delays the individual maturation of each twin into adulthood.[5]

Competition and Comparison
Envy and competition are magnified in twins. Twins are routinely compared and contrasted with each other growing up, sometimes in a well-meaning fashion by relatives and friends: "Oh, you're the quiet one, right? And you're the life of the party, I can tell!" Given that they have been consistently compared to their same-age sibling, twins have the understandable sense that they are always being measured against someone else. Also, as adults, any change or new situation for one twin can trigger intense feelings of jealousy, insecurity, or self-doubt in the other.

Accommodation
The degree of accommodation that goes on between twins is vastly more pronounced than between singleton siblings, and it profoundly impacts their individual identity. A twin feels guilty if he doesn't accommodate his needs to his twin's, thinks of himself instead of his twin, or accomplishes something that his twin cannot or does not accomplish.

Push-Pull of Twin Closeness versus Self-Definition
Twins' closeness, caretaking/cared-for dynamic, and collaborative functioning is often in conflict with their desire to become independent of each other and to figure out who they are as individuals. While they may experience an ongoing pull toward the twin connection and a feeling that they are lost without their twin, there is also a natural struggle toward developing an individual identity. The conflict between these two opposing inclinations can result in intense anxiety or depression.

Living in a "Twin Bubble"
Being overly dependent on one's twin can produce a kind of inertia or stasis. Too much togetherness often has a crippling effect, as it may breed a laziness founded on the ongoing belief that one is unable to do things alone. In adult twins, this may inhibit resilience and lead them to

make certain life choices that are safe and predictable, rather than doing things that are challenging and more rewarding.

Inability to Acknowledge Negative Feelings

Because twins are brought up in a culture that believes twins are soul mates who should always get along and be best friends forever, they are often unable to acknowledge negative feelings or conflict between the two of them. And they may feel terrible guilt when they do so. If they become involved in twin-like relationships with friends or lovers, this dynamic can present itself in a similar manner.

Fighting between Twins

When twins come to therapy because they're fighting, the therapist needs to remember that twins always have the expectation that they should never fight. So they think of fighting as a terrible thing. They often don't have the capacity to understand why they're fighting, and they also don't know how to manage their differences. Ruptures over little matters can seem magnified because of their inability to feel like they are two separate people who disagree. They will need help from the therapist to unravel their symbiotic paralysis. Sometimes their differences are indeed irreconcilable and the two may need to have little contact with each other. However, whereas a married couple who are fighting may reach the point where divorce seems to be the only solution, twins who can't get along are still related. Some twins are happy to have nothing to do with each other, but because they remain siblings, a complete "divorce" is more profound.

Fear of Closeness

Some twins who have grown up too closely connected may avoid or fear closeness in their adult relationships. They may feel impinged upon by friends or lovers because growing up as a twin robbed them of a single self that they are now careful to preserve and protect.

Inflated Sense of Being Special

The feeling of being special is fueled by twin identity. The desire to be special often masks a sense of fragility or an immature self. Feeling entitled to special care and attention can be part of a twin's identity and can engender a narcissistic quality. Kate Bacon is an identical twin and the author of *Twins in Society*. From her sociological perspective, she writes about twins having access to social status and social capital (broader social networks):

> The temptation to move back into aspects of twinship seems to increase in adulthood. No longer expected to be "twins," adults may cling on to aspects of twin identity to reaffirm their status as twins. . . . Female twins in particular may be more able to cling on to aspects of twinship and the symbolic and social capital potentially available through playing up closeness, because expressions of twin closeness fall in line with discourses of femininity.[6]

Twinship Experienced as Traumatic

Many twins come to therapy experiencing or having experienced traumatic circumstances due to their twinship. I don't think most people associate twinship with trauma, but having treated twin clients for decades, I can attest to the fact that certain aspects of being a twin can result in traumatic experiences. For example, for a caretaker twin to be compelled to give up her caretaking role, to no longer be able to function in a way that defines her identity, can be profoundly frightening and disturbing. A twin therapist must understand that what a twin is going through in such a circumstance is most certainly a traumatic experience.

Twin Loss

Losing a twin is much more complicated in terms of mourning and grief than losing a singleton sibling. The process usually goes on for a longer period of time, as it is less like losing a brother or sister and more like losing a part of yourself.

More Twins, More Twin Therapists Needed

According to research by the Centers for Disease Control and Prevention, as referenced by Nancy Segal in her book *Twin Mythconceptions*,

> The advent of assisted reproduction over the last 30–40 years has dramatically increased the overall twinning rate (both identical and fraternal), from nearly 1 in 60 births (18.9/1000) in 1980 to over 1 in 30 births (33.7/1000) in 2013.
> ... While the twinning rate is the highest it has ever been, the highest number of twins born in the United States was 138,961 in 2007.... In 2013, in the United States, multiples accounted for 43.6% of [assisted-reproduction]-conceived infants.[7]

With more twins in the population, more therapists are needed who are knowledgeable in the treatment of twin-related issues. Of course, not all twins have problems that require therapy. In fact, more twins than not get along.

When I talk to twins groups about twinship issues that I help clients deal with in my practice, someone will usually come up to me after my presentation and say something like "Oh my gosh, I love my twin, we talk every day, we have a special bond, and now I feel so lucky! None of those things that you were talking about ever comes up for us! I had no idea that there are twins who have trouble getting along. It never crossed my mind."

Like that twins group participant, many twins have harmonious relationships and have not found that growing up a twin has negatively impacted their sense of individuality or their relationships with others. Some twins are friends and their relationship is essentially no different than relationships between singleton siblings. And others may have had issues with their twin but have found ways to get along. Some twins may not see each other that often or may not be that close but experience no serious problems between them, no animosity or conflicts, and no negative repercussions as a result of being a twin.

This broad population of twins whose twinship does not present significant difficulties is generally not reflected in my practice. Twins who seek my help are those who have problems sorting through one or more of the various issues we have been exploring throughout this book. And it is this diverse group of twins that you will likely encounter in your practice.

Being a twin therapist has been my life's work, and I have found it tremendously fulfilling. Listening as twins open up to me about their twinship experiences, their struggles and aspirations, has been a privilege and an education. It has greatly expanded my understanding of the unique psychological environment that twins inhabit. It has been my honor to help clients deal with those difficulties as they chart their own path toward developing a singular self. And I hope that you will find the experience of treating twins equally rewarding.

Notes

Chapter 1

1. Bethany Saltman, "Can Attachment Theory Explain All Our Relationships?" The Cut, July 5, 2016, http://www.thecut.com/2016/06/attachment-theory-motherhood-c-v-r.html.

2. D. W. Winnicott, *Through Paediatrics to Psycho-analysis* (London: Hogarth Press, 1958), 301–3.

3. Saltman, "Attachment Theory."

4. Beatrice Beebe and Frank M. Lachmann, *Infant Research and Adult Treatment: Co-constructing Interactions* (Hillsdale, NJ: Analytic Press, 2005), 15.

5. Beebe and Lachman, 225–26.

6. Ruth Simon, "There Is No Such Thing as a Baby: Early Psychic Development in Twins," *Contemporary Psychoanalysis* 52, no. 3 (2016): 363, doi:10.1080/00107530.2016.1169906.

7. Simon, 369.

8. Simon, 366.

9. Kate Bacon, *Twins in Society: Parents, Bodies, Space and Talk* (Basingstoke, UK: Palgrave Macmillan, 2010) 48–49.

10. Vivienne Lewin, *The Twin Enigma* (London: Karnac Books 2016), 9.

11. Audrey C. Sandbank, "Personality, Identity and Family Relationships," in *Twin and Triplet Psychology: A Professional Guide to Working with Multiples*, ed. Audrey C. Sandbank (London: Routledge, 1999), 167–68.

12. Simon, "No Such Thing," 370.

Chapter 2

1. E. D. Joseph and J. H. Tabor, "The Simultaneous Analysis of a Pair of Identical Twins and the Twinning Reaction," *Psychoanalytic Study of the Child* 16 (1961): 277, quoted in Elizabeth A. Stewart, *Exploring Twins: Towards a Social Analysis of Twinship* (Basingstoke, UK: Palgrave Macmillan, 2003), 69.
2. Stewart, *Exploring Twins*, 69.
3. Stewart, 70.
4. Barbara Klein, *Alone in the Mirror: Twins in Therapy* (New York: Routledge, 2012), 115.

Chapter 3

1. Klein, *Alone in the Mirror*, 70.
2. Stewart, *Exploring Twins*, 33.
3. Lewin, *Twin Enigma*, 99.

Chapter 4

1. Shelley R. Doctors, "Brandchaft's Pathological Accommodation —What It Is and What It Isn't," *Psychoanalysis, Self and Context* 12, no. 1 (2017): 48.
2. Doctors, 46–47.

Chapter 5

1. Dale H. Ortmeyer, "The We-Self of Identical Twins," *Contemporary Psychoanalysis* 6, no. 2 (1970): 125, quoted in Stewart, *Exploring Twins*, 70.
2. Vivienne Lewin, *The Twin in the Transference* (Philadelphia: Whurr, 2004), 126–27.

Chapter 6

1. Sandbank, "Personality, Identity and Relationships," 182.

2. Joan A. Friedman, *The Same but Different: How Twins Can Live, Love, and Learn to Be Individuals* (Los Angeles: Rocky Pines Press, 2014).

Chapter 7

1. Sirpa Pietilä, Pia Bülow, and Anita Björklund, "Twinship and Marriage—Experiences during the Course of Twin Relationships," *Review of European Studies* 4, no. 4 (2012): 52, http://www.ccsenet.org/journal/index.php/res/article/viewFile/19476/12911.

2. Pietilä, Bülow, and Björklund, 45.

Chapter 8

1. Philip M. Bromberg, "Standing in the Spaces: The Multiplicity of Self and the Psychoanalytic Relationship," *Contemporary Psychoanalysis* 32 (1996): 509–35.

2. Jessica Benjamin, "Beyond Doer and Done To: An Intersubjective View of Thirdness," *Psychoanalytic Quarterly* 73, no. 1 (2004): 5–46.

3. Susan Fisher, "The Metaphor of Twinship in Personality Development," *British Journal of Psychotherapy* 2, no. 4 (June 1986): 271–80.

4. Winnicott, *Through Paediatrics to Psycho-analysis*, 301–3.

5. Lewin, *Twin Enigma*, 38.

6. Bacon, *Twins in Society*, 193.

7. Nancy L. Segal, *Twin Mythconceptions: False Beliefs, Fables, and Facts about Twins* (London: Elsevier, 2017), 2–3.

Index

A

abandonment issues
  confronting, 37–42
  depression and, 38–42
  effects on relationship of, 75
  of left-behind twin, 120–121
  in separation process, 22
  shame for having, 41–42
  and significant others, 68–71, 85
  of spouse, 138–139
abusive relationships, 19, 87, 90–92, 97
accommodation between twins, 73–74, 162
accomplishments, 93–94
adjustment issues, 1–2, 21, 38–42
anger, 22, 58–61, 112
anxiety
  ability to handle, 95
  causes of, 91, 93, 151, 152, 162
  creation of acute, 89
  going to college, 1–2, 21
  in individuation process, 113
  in older nontwin siblings, 72
  panic attacks, 92, 94, 108, 121–122, 161
  as presenting problem, 22
  separation-induced, 2, 18
  social, 23, 47, 63
  of spouse/partner, 134
arguments. *See* conflict/disagreements
attachment formation
  caretaker role of child in, 72–73
  conflicting attachments, 145–148
  difficulty with, 23
  to fathers, 14–16
  friendship as, 77–78
  importance of, 159–160
  parent-twin, 48
  preference for one twin over the other, 12–13
  to twin versus parent, 159
attachment history, 16–17
attachment-individuation process, 4
attachments, conflicting, 145–148
attachment theory, 2–5
authentic/inauthentic feelings, 23, 24, 124
autonomy, 1–2, 4–5. *See also* separate self

B

Bacon, Kate, 9, 164
bad twin. *See* good twin/bad twin dynamic
Beebe, Beatrice, 4
Benjamin, Jessica, 158
Björklund, Anita, 145
black-and-white thinking, 63–65
blame, 51
boundaries, 127–130
Bowlby, John, 2–3
boyfriends. *See* significant others
Brandchaft, Bernard, 73
Bromberg, Philip, 158
Bülow, Pia, 145

C

caretaker/cared-for dynamic
  caretaking of friends, 76–78
  child as caretaker for parent, 72
  denying needed help in, 81–83
  dominant/passive labels in, 83–84
  duplication in outside relationships of, 125
  effects of, 49–50
  emotional, 115
  emotionally disconnecting in, 74–76
  identification of, 152, 153
  mutual caretaking, 27
  with other siblings, 98–99
  pathological accommodation in, 72–74
  reasons for, 67–68
  renouncing the, 84–86
  sacrifice, 68–71
  of twin and married twin, 135
  twins' perception of, 23
  unreciprocated selflessness in, 78–80
categorization and labeling of twins, 63–65, 83

Centers for Disease Control, 165
change
    acceptance without, 122
    baby steps for, 78
    effects of, 41–42, 162
    facing, 38–42
    going to college, 1–2, 21
    motivation for, 35
    personal, 94
    to twin dynamic, 62, 114, 138, 142, 145
closeness. *See* intimacy/closeness
co-construction, 4, 154–156
communication between twins, 44, 95–96
comparisons
    competition and, 162
    in good twin/bad twin dynamic, 49
    internalization of, 50
    labeling, categorizing, 63–65
    singletons and twin siblings, 63–64
    to twin, 111
competition
    comparisons and, 162
    finding a partner outside the twinship, 122–123
    relationships based on, 113
    between twins, 111
complementarity, 88–91
conflict/disagreements
    acceptance of, 119
    agreeing to disagree, 33–34
    avoidance of, 74, 77
    couples' conflicts, 23, 33–34,
    discussing, 118
    emotional investment in, 35–36
    exploring, 101–102
    fear of, 32, 116
    in friendships, 114–116
    guilt about, 31
    inability to acknowledge, 163
    lack of, 165
    loyalty, 61
    in outside friendships, 113–116
    in replacement relationships, 117–120, 124–125
    separation-related, 90
    with spouse, 133
    between twins, 23
    uncontrollable anger, 22
    See also good twin/bad twin dynamic
conflicting attachments, 145–148
connections
    expectations for outside-of-twinship, 123
    loss of, 109–113

connections *(continued)*
    mother-baby, 4
    to self, 94–98
    sense of twin, 134
    understanding of, by significant others, 145–146
core self, 27
couples' conflicts, 23, 33–34

D

dating issues, 140–142
dependence/interdependence, 27–28, 35, 109. *See also* replacement relationships; separate self
dependence on one's twin, 87–88
depression, 22, 38–42, 79, 162
development process, 3–4
disagreements. *See* conflict/disagreements
disparaged twin identity, 98–102, 107
Doctors, Shelley R., 73–74
dominance
    in caretaker/cared-for dynamic, 83–84
    dominant twin, 117–120
    by spouse, 21, 119

E

emotional equilibrium, 24, 35–36
emotional investment, 34–36
emotions/feelings
    anger, 22, 58–61, 112
    authentic/inauthentic, 23, 124
    depression, 22, 38–42, 79, 162
    disconnecting from, 74–76
    expression of, 57, 97
    merging of twins' separate, 33
    negative, 119, 163
    nurturing of, 115
    overreacting to others', 95
    processing of, 87, 114
    sharing of, 116
    validation of, 42–44
empathy
    effects of, 44
    lack of, 49, 70–71
    learning, 10
    overempathizing, 73
    therapist's, 151
    for understanding the other, 61–62, 65
entitlement issues, 82
envy/jealousy, 22, 54–57, 64, 157, 162
expectations, 23, 80, 123, 125

Index

F
fathers, twin attachment to, 14–16
favoritism, 12–13, 15, 48, 58, 68
feelings. *See* emotions/feelings
fighting between twins, 163
Fisher, Susan, 159
Freud, Sigmund, 154
friends/friendships
    avoidance of, 125
    caretaking of, 76–78
    compared to twinship, 114–115
    conflicts in, 114–116
    outside of twin relationship, 47–48, 68–72, 113–116, 130–134
    in triadic relationships, 54–57
fused identity, 30, 120–124

G
girlfriends. *See* significant others
"going on being" state, 3
good twin/bad twin dynamic, 48
    bad twin to singular self, 52–54
    black-and-white thinking and, 63–65
    in classic mythology, 53
    getting to know each other in, 61–63
    from good twin to bad twin, 54–57
    problem child versus successful child, 49–52
    righteous anger of bad twin, 58–61
    stereotypes in film/television, 52
    triad situations, 56
guilt
    acknowledging negative feelings and, 163
    in crises of identity, 108
    guilt-tripping, 56
    separation and, 161
    sources of, 22
    for success, 101

H
husbands. *See* marriage issues; significant others

I
identity
    comfort with singular, 124
    confronting turmoil about, 91–94
    confusion of self and other, 28
    creation of new, 130
    crises of, 96, 107–108
    desire to be special and, 164
    disparaged twin, 98–102
    formation of twins', 2
    fused, 30, 120–124
    as good or bad twin, 48–49

identity *(continued)*
    merged, 95–96, 102–107
    push-pull of developing, 162
    relationship-based, 112–113
    reliance on twinship for, 31
    self-connection, 94–98
    as a twin, 40
    we-self, 88–91
inauthentic/authentic feelings, 23, 24, 124
independence. *See* separation
infantilization, 49
infants, 2–5, 7, 8
insecurity/security, 54–57, 64–65, 73
interdependence/dependence, 27–28, 35, 109. *See also* replacement relationships; separate self
intimacy/closeness
    avoidance of, 127
    development of, 18
    expectation of, 23
    fear of, 163
    losing the dynamic of, 122
    in outside friendships, 20, 27, 32
    with spouse versus twin, 133, 147
    threats to, 156
    unwanted, 124

J
jealousy/envy, 22, 54–57, 64, 157, 162
Joseph, E. D., 27–28, 32

K
Klein, Barbara, 45, 48
Kohut, Heinz, 154

L
labeling and categorization of twins, 63–65, 83
Lachmann, Frank M., 4
Lewin, Vivienne, 10, 53, 88–89, 161
loathing, self-, 22
loss of a twin, 41, 164
loyalty, 61, 135–136, 137, 138, 144, 148
Lyons-Ruth, Karlen, 4

M
marriage issues
    abuse, 87
    benefits of twinship relationship, 147
    boundaries, 127–130
    caretaking dynamic, 153
    changes to the twin dynamic, 122
    comparisons to twinship, 145
    conflict with spouse, 133

marriage issues *(continued)*
  demands of spouse over one's twin, 135–140
  dominance by wife, 119
  expectations of twin by spouse, 137
  friendship between spouses, 123
  judgment of, by one's twin, 128–129
  obligations/loyalty, 144
  outside twin as intruder, 134
  overprotectiveness of twin, 115
  replacement of twin, 120–124
  role confusion, 142–143
  spouse's perspectives, 21, 138
  threats to marriage, 20–21, 114, 147
  threats to twinship, 119–128
  validation from spouse, 130–134
  See also significant others
maternal preoccupation, 3
merged identities, 95–96, 102–107
mirroring, 27, 31, 159–160
mother-child attachment
  attachment theory, 2–5
  dyadic mental hold of mother in, 7
  preference for one twin over the other, 12–13, 48
  research on adult problems of, 3–4
  with two babies, 5–8
mutual recognition, 156–158

N
needs
  accommodation of, 77, 125, 162
  emotional, 5–6, 85
  fear of articulating, 119–120
  focusing on one's twin's, 160
  honoring one's own, 78
  identification of, 18, 97, 108
  neglect by one's twin of, 82, 141–142
  parental focus on, 10, 12–14
  sacrificing one's, 83, 86, 101
  suppression of, 24
  therapeutic, 37
  twin's sensitivity to others', 72
negative feelings, 119, 163
nontwin siblings
  anxiety in, 72
  caretaker/cared-for dynamic of, 98–99
  closeness of significant others to, 147–148
  comparison between twin and, 63–64
  parenting of, 98–102
nonverbal communication, 44, 95–96

O
Ortmeyer, Dale, 88–89

P
panic, 2, 22, 92, 94, 108, 121–122, 161. *See also* anxiety
parents/parenting
  abusive, 91–92
  of caretaking twins, 85–86
  comparing same-age children, 50–51
  inadequate nurturing, 34
  labeling/categorizing by, 63–64
  of other siblings, 98–102
  primary maternal preoccupation, 3, 5–6
  reverse, 72–74
  second parents, 14–16, 91–92
  turmoil of, 94–95
  validation as role of, 26–28, 31
partners. *See* marriage issues; significant others
passive/submissive twins, 84
pathological accommodation, 73–74
personhood, 156
perspectives
  objective/subjective, 70–71, 81
  of spouse/significant other, 21, 138, 144, 147–148
  twins' differing, 153–154
  on twinship dynamic, 24
Pietilä, Sirpa, 145
primary maternal preoccupation, 3
  with two babies, 5–6
"problem child" label, 49–52
push-pull of twin closeness, 162

Q
quarreling, 31–33

R
rage, 23
reality checks, 70
rebellion, 58–61, 65
recognition, mutual, 156–158
relatedness, for achieving autonomy, 4–5
relationality, 154–156
relationships
  abusive, 87, 90–92, 97
  comparisons of twin/outside, 114–115
  confusion in, 111
  deterioration of, 30
  establishing, 44
  friendship (*see* friends/friendships)
  reasons for problematic, 43
  replacement (*see* replacement relationships)

relationships *(continued)*
  romantic *(see* marriage issues; significant others)
  structure of twinship, 92
  symbiotic, 27
  twinship as benefit to marriage, 145–146

R

replacement relationships, 113–116
  common scenarios in, 124–125
  fused identity and, 120–124
  loss of connection and, 109–113
  See also marriage issues; significant others
resentment, 49–50
responsibility for behavior, 51, 53–54
reverse parenting, 72–74
rivalry, 67
roles
  acceptability to others of twinship's, 145
  acting as conscience, 88–89
  being stuck in, 33
  breaking out of, 101–102
  caretaker *(see* caretaker/cared-for dynamic)
  choosing, 75–76
  confusion of, 142–144
  in dyads, 2
  of each twin, 24
  exploration of, 92
  influence of favoritism on, 58
  parental, 27
  problem child/successful child, 49–52
  of therapist, 36–37
  unwanted, 117
romantic relationships. *See* marriage issues; significant others
Romulus and Remus myth, 53

S

sacrifice, 68–72, 80, 83, 86, 101
Saltman, Bethany, 3
second parents, 14–16, 91–92
security/insecurity, 54–57, 64–65, 73
Segal, Nancy, 165
self-definition struggle, 34, 76, 162
self-disclosure, 155–156
self-esteem, development of, 27
selflessness
  unreciprocated, 78–80
  See also caretaker/cared-for dynamic
self-loathing, 22
self-perception of twins, 23–24
self-preservation, 75
self-sharing, 120
self-states, 96, 158–159
"self with other" model, 154

self-worth, 51
separate self, 102–107
  anxiety and panic attacks in separation process, 113
  attempts to establish, 51
  authentic, 36
  experience of, 24
  first experience of autonomy, 1–2
  quarreling as means to, 31–33
  successful development of, 45–56
  See also interdependence/dependence
separation
  acceptable, 163
  after marriage, 131
  benefits of, 83
  effects on relationship of, 90
  expressing feelings about, 43
  guilt and, 161
  left-behind twin, 120–121
  loss of companionship and, 40–41
  in middle age, 28
  panic and, 161
  relatedness versus, 4–5
    for achieving autonomy, 4–5
separation anxiety, 2
shame
  overcoming, 42–44
  over sense of loss, 41
  twinship-related, 23
  validation of, 42–43
shared self, 120
siblings. *See* nontwin siblings
significant others
  abandonment issues of outside twin, 41–42, 68–71, 85
  abusive, 19, 87, 90–92, 97
  adjusting to, 38–42
  anxiety in, 134, 141
  breakups with, 28, 29, 43, 79, 80
  caretaking roles, 74
  closeness between one's twin and, 147–148
  erecting new boundaries with, 127–130
  expectations of, 140–141
  overinvolved twins with, 135–140
  reaction of one's twin to new, 68–72
  relationships with other family members, 55–56
  twin versus, 127
  validation from, 130–134
  See also marriage issues
Simon, Ruth, 5–7, 14, 15, 16
singular self, 52, 96–97, 124

social anxiety, 23
social capital, 164
specialness, 164
spouses. *See* marriage issues; significant others
stepparents. *See* second parents
Stewart, Elizabeth, 28, 52
Stockholm syndrome, 142
submissive/passive twins, 84
"successful child" label, 49–52
suicidal thoughts, 59, 61–62, 65
symbiotic paralysis, 163
symbiotic relationships, 27
synergy, 28–31

T

Tabor, J. H., 27
teenagers, 58–61
temperament, 4
therapeutic issues with twins
    caretaker/cared-for twins, 77–78, 84–86
    causes of depression, 61–62
    common themes in, 160–164
    couples therapy for, 44–46
    defining oneself, 65
    effects of prior therapy, 90
    elements of psychology of twins, 23–24
    envy/jealousy, 22, 57
    exploring conflict, 101–102
    expressing anger, 112
    familiarity with issues of, 149–151
    in good twin/bad twin dynamic, 52–54
    hostility of spouse, 135–140
    improving relationships, 62–63
    learning about twinship issues, 151–154
    mutual recognition in, 156–158
    need for therapists, 165–166
    presenting issues of twins, 20–24
    relationality and co-construction, 154–156
    replacement relationship conflicts, 120, 124–125
    role conflicts, 143–144
    seeking validation from significant others, 130–134

therapeutic issues with twins *(continued)*
    self-disclosure, 155–156
    self-states in, 158–159
    therapist-patient dyads, 155
    transference issues, 17–20
    twin versus parental mirroring in, 159–160
    unrealistic expectations of twins, 80
therapeutic validation, 36–37
therapy models, 154–155
traumatic experience of twinship, 164
triadic relationships, 48, 54–57, 141
turmoil, confronting, 91–94
twin bubble, 162–163
twin-like relationships. *See* replacement relationships
twin mystique, 29–30
twinning rates in United States, 165
twinning reaction, 27–28
twin preoccupation, 159
twinship dynamic
    outside perspectives on, 24
    siblings as part of, 98–102
    as team, 122
twin-to-twin attachment, 8–11
two-person therapy, 154

U

upbringing, 160–161

V

validation
    of feelings, 42–44
    inadequate, 26–28
    parental, 31
    from spouse, 130–134
    therapeutic, 36–37
victimhood, 50–51, 64

W

we-self mentality, 88–91, 94
Winnicott, Donald, 3, 160
wives. *See* marriage issues; significant others

About the Author

Dr. Joan A. Friedman is a gifted psychotherapist who has devoted many years of her professional career to educating twins and their families about twins' emotional needs. Having worked through her own twinship challenges and parented her fraternal twin sons, she is a definitive expert on twin development.

She is the author of *Emotionally Healthy Twins: A New Philosophy for Parenting Two Unique Children* and *The Same but Different: How Twins Can Live, Love, and Learn to Be Individuals*. She has spoken to and consulted with culturally diverse groups of twins around the world. Dr. Friedman's work focuses on issues that adult twins confront as they adjust to life as singletons after having been raised as twins.

You can reach Dr. Friedman via
LinkedIn: bit.ly/2i36T6V
Facebook: www.facebook.com/joanafriedmanphd
Twitter: twitter.com/Joanafriedman
Website: www.joanafriedmanphd.com